MORE TEN-MINUTE PLAYS

from

Actors Theatre of Louisville

Foreword by
Jon Jory

Edited by
Michael Bigelow Dixon

IMPORTANT BILLING AND CREDIT REQUIREMENTS

All producers of any play in this volume *must* give credit to the Author of the Play in all programs distributed in connection with performances of the Play and in all instances in which the title of the Play appears for purposes of advertising, publicizing or otherwise exploiting the Play and/or a production. The name of the Author *must* also appear on a separate line, on which no other name appears, immediately following the title, and *must* appear in size of type not less than fifty percent the size of the title type.

iv

TABLE OF CONTENTS

FOREWORD

Here they are, twenty-six more short plays from Louisville, exemplifying the temper of the times. After years of the literature of Freudian revelation and decades of the television sit-com, problem drama, and social commentary of the week, we've developed an emotional shorthand which these plays suit perfectly. Bam! A page to set the situation. Crash! A few character details. Wham! The obstacle. And, Shazam, the resolution.

Do I satirize the form? Not really. With almost every dramatic situation inspiring a sense of *déjà vu* in the reader or audience, we almost bring the first two acts into the theatre unspoken and arrive ready for the climax. The ten-minute play thus has the audience's previous experiences as exposition and can move directly on to the telling gesture, the obligatory scene or the atmospheric metaphor.

Here, as well, there is no room for the luxury of narrative, or the novel's rich digression, or the long play's accretion of detail. Here the smallest thing must signify and sticking to the point is crucial.

This makes the ten-minute form particularly valuable as a teaching tool. If the sculptor finds the form in the marble and simply chips away all else, then the actor, director, and designer must eschew decoration or artistic plaque in dealing with the mini-play. Here you must personalize the central and do only that. How valuable this skill will be to addressing the masterpieces, a Hamlet, a Hedda, where finding the center is salvation!

These twenty-six works plumb the center of relationships, issues, and character in many styles and intents. Sometimes they even pursue the perfect joke. They are the haiku of the theatre and can evoke the same pleasure.

At their best they are perfect single gestures of theatricality and language.

Jon Jory
Producing Director
Actors Theatre of Louisville

LYNETTE AT 3 AM

by
Jane Anderson

Lynette at 3 AM is the co-winner of the Actors Theatre of Louisville 1991 National Ten-Minute Play Contest and the Heideman Award.

Lynette at 3 AM premiered at the Actors Theatre of Louisville on June 17, 1991. It was directed by Reid Davis. The cast was:

LYNETTE ....Kristen Harris
BOBBY ....Michael David Weis
ESTABAN ....Jesse Wolfe

Scenic Design: Paul Owen
Costume Designer: Kevin McLeod
Lighting Designer: Matt Reinert
Sound Designer: Darron West
Production Manager: Bob Krakower
Stage Manager: Emily Fox
Dramaturgs: Deborah Frockt
Property Master: Mark Bissonnette

CHARACTERS

LYNETTE—who's had trouble sleeping lately.

BOBBY—her boyfriend. A very large man who works too hard.

ESTABAN—from the apartment below.

TIME
Present

PLACE
An Apartment in Brooklyn

LYNETTE AT 3 AM

THREE A.M. Lynette's apartment in Brooklyn.
LYNETTE is lying awake on the bed with BOBBY, who's fast
asleep.
We hear the TOILET running.
We hear traffic.
We hear a car alarm. It stops.
Very faintly, we hear something that sounds like a GUN SHOT.
LYNETTE sits up and listens.

LYNETTE. Bobby. Bobby, wake up.
BOBBY. Uh.
LYNETTE. I heard a gun go off.
BOBBY. (*Still asleep.*) Where?
LYNETTE. I think in the building somewhere.
BOBBY. Where in the building?
LYNETTE. I think maybe the apartment below.
BOBBY. So what do you want me to do about it?
LYNETTE. You want to call the police?
BOBBY. You call. You're the one who heard it.

(A beat.)

LYNETTE. You wanna maybe check in the hall, see if there's
anything out there?
BOBBY. What's gonna be in the hall?
LYNETTE. I just thought maybe you should check.
BOBBY. There's nothing to check in the hall. Anything to see
would be behind a door. There's no point to the hall. The hall has
nothing.
LYNETTE. OK.
BOBBY. If you think you heard an actual gun, if you are
certain you heard it, then make the commitment and call the police.

9

But don't say you're not sure and make me get up and go to the hall. That's not what I'm here for. I'm not interested in that.

LYNETTE. OK. *(A beat.)* I just have this funny feeling.

BOBBY. You always get paranoid in the middle of the night

LYNETTE. If it were a gun then there'd be people yelling. There'd be commotion, right? *(A beat.)* Maybe it was just a car making a backfire on the street. Or maybe a cat knocked a book offa someone's shelf. You think that's it?

BOBBY. Mmm.

LYNETTE. That's probably it. *(A beat.)* Bobby?

BOBBY. Wha.

LYNETTE. Hold me?

(BOBBY rolls over on his back so Lynette can lay on him. HE flops his arm over her and falls back to sleep.

BOBBY. Sorry.

(BOBBY goes back to sleep. LYNETTE lays her head on his chest.)

(We hear Bobby's HEART BEAT. HE snores slightly. LYNETTE jiggles him to stop. SHE listens to his HEARTBEAT: It beats, stops for a moment then starts up again.)

(LYNETTE sits up, panicked.)

LYNETTE. Bobby, Bobby.

BOBBY. Uh.

LYNETTE. Bobby wake up.

BOBBY. Wha.

LYNETTE. Your heart stopped. I heard it.

BOBBY. No it didn't.

LYNETTE. Bobby, it did.

BOBBY. We don't have heart in my family. We have cancer, we don't have heart.

LYNETTE. I swear to God. I was listening very specifically. I was counting the beats.

BOBBY. What were you counting the beats for?

LYNETTE. Because I love you.

BOBBY. Jesus.

LYNETTE. I love that even though you're sleeping, this little part of you is still awake, working to keep you alive. I think that's a miracle, don't you?

BOBBY. C'mon, Lynette, I gotta get up early.

(BOBBY turns over.)

LYNETTE. Bobby, when you get up to pee in the middle of the night do you ever think about your own death?

BOBBY. No.

LYNETTE. While I was sitting on the toilet I touched the top of my knees and I thought about how someday everything will be rotted away and there will only be bones there. And there will be no point to shaving my legs anymore because there will be no skin on which to support the hair. And it occurred to me that even the act of urination is not a forever kind of thing and it's something I should treasure because someday my bladder will turn to dust. *(BOBBY lets out an impatient breath.)* Breathing. This is also a special thing. Lungs are not forever. Someday they'll be two dried sponges.

BOBBY. Shit, Lynette, Shit.

LYNETTE. I'm sorry.

BOBBY. I'll be fucked if I don't get my sleep. C'mon.

LYNETTE. I know. I'm sorry.

BOBBY. *(Overlap.)* Three hours, I gotta get up …

LYNETTE. *(Overlap.)* I know. Go to sleep. I want you to sleep. Good night.

(LYNETTE lays down. SHE changes position. SHE changes position again.)

BOBBY. Stop it.

LYNETTE. Could we spoon?

BOBBY. Jesus.

LYNETTE. Never mind.
BOBBY. All right.

(THEY readjust positions. BOBBY wraps himself around Lynette. A beat.)

LYNETTE. Are you still in love with me?
BOBBY. Why are you asking me this?
LYNETTE. Because usually when we spoon you get a hard-on.
BOBBY. Jesus, Lynette …
LYNETTE. Sorry. *(A beat.)* But you still love me?

(No response.)

(LYNETTE settles down. A beat. BOBBY snores very faintly.
A car with a SCRAPING MUFFLER passes by.
Silence.
The PIPES in the building thud a few times.
Silence.
LYNETTE sits up. SHE takes the remote from the bedside table and turns on the TV. SHE immediately mutes the sound and just stares at the picture.
A beat.
ESTABAN a young Latino MAN appears. HE is barefoot and dressed in a white T-shirt and white pants.
LYNETTE stares at him.)

ESTABAN. Hello. My name is Estaban. I'm from the apartment below. I just died.
LYNETTE. Oh my God.
ESTABAN. I am sorry to disturb you. I have to pass through so I can go … *(HE points up.)* … to above.
LYNETTE. Was this like a few minutes ago this happened?
ESTABAN. Yes.
LYNETTE. I thought I heard a gun. Was that you?
ESTABAN. Yes.
LYNETTE. You know, I knew there was something. I told

Bobby, I said to him there was definitely a shot. So that was you?

ESTABAN. That was me.

LYNETTE. I was gonna call the police. Should I call the police?

ESTABAN. It doesn't matter anymore.

LYNETTE. Who shot you?

ESTABAN. My brother Jorge.

LYNETTE. Oh my God, your brother?

ESTABAN. I was making love to his wife.

LYNETTE. Oh. Well. That wasn't a smart thing to be doing.

ESTABAN. It couldn't be helped. Lola and me, we fell in love when we were fifteen.

LYNETTE. Really? So this has been going on a long time then.

ESTABAN. Yes. Me and Lola, we grew up in the same village in Puerto Rico.

LYNETTE. I hear Puerto Rico is a nice place to vacation. Is it nice there?

ESTABAN. Like a paradise.

LYNETTE. I've always wanted to see the islands. But Bobby, he's not a traveller.

ESTABAN. No?

LYNETTE. But you and Lola, I want to hear about. So you met on the island, you were soul mates, go on.

ESTABAN. The first time we made love it was siesta time. We walked down the street, everyone was asleep. Everything was quiet except for the waves flipping over very soft. It was hot, just a little bit windy from the ocean. Very sexy. I took her to the shade of a vanilla bean tree. We lay down on a blanket. She opened her blouse for me and her skin, it smelled sweet just like the tree. After we made love, I cried.

LYNETTE. I do that too. I cry after Bobby and me make love. So you cry too?

ESTABAN. Oh yes. It is because when I make love, my heart leaves my body for heaven. And when it is over and my heart has to come back, it is very sad.

LYNETTE. See, my crying thing is a little different. When I make love and my heart leaves my body I'm always expecting to meet Bobby's heart outside his body. But Bobby's heart—well

Bobby has a hard time opening up, if you met his family you'd understand.His heart doesn't really leave his body. so my heart is out there all alone waiting while Bobby finishes up. Below. And then he falls asleep and I'm still out there, floating and feeling very lonely. And then I cry and wake Bobby up and he gets annoyed. Which is not to say that I don't get a lot of other things from him.

ESTABAN. Yes?

LYNETTE. So how come Lola didn't marry you?

ESTABAN. Her parents said, "Lola, marry Jorge he make better money than Estaban."

LYNETTE. Aw, that's not fair.

ESTABAN. That is life. Jorge, he runs a car service to the airport. I been working for him. Olmos Limo.

LYNETTE. I hate to fly. I see my own death when I fly.

ESTABAN. See, when I drive someone to the airport I always say before they get out "have a safe trip, God bless." Not one of my passengers ever died in a plane crash. It's part of the service.

LYNETTE. That's nice. (A beat.) So do you know where you're going? Is anyone gonna be meeting you, like do you have grandparents or anyone who're gonna take you over to the other side?

ESTABAN. No, all my family's still alive.

LYNETTE. Are you Catholic?

ESTABAN. Yeah, I grew up with that.

LYNETTE. Do you think the Virgin Mary will be there?

ESTABAN. I don't know.

LYNETTE. Did you go through a tunnel and see a white light?

ESTABEN. No, I haven't even left the building yet.

LYNETTE. Are you scared?

ESTABAN. What's to be scared? It's nature. Everything dies. Chickens and dogs and pussy cats and movie stars and cockroaches, and grandmommies and guys like me who drive people to the airport. We all gotta do it. So how can something that everybody has to do be so bad?

LYNETTE. But you think there's something to go to? You think there's something else?

ESTABAN. Sure, why not?

LYNETTE. Bobby says all of that stuff is bullshit, that when you die you die.

ESTABAN. Oh man, don't listen to him. How can a guy who can't make good love know anything about the afterlife. Geez, no wonder you're such a scared lady.

LYNETTE. I didn't paint a fair picture. He's a very good person.

ESTABAN. What's your name?

LYNETTE. Lynette.

ESTABAN. Ay, Lynetta, Lynetta. *Tu eres muy amable y muy hermosa. Deseo que te pudiera besarte y tener tus cenos en mis manos como si fueran frutas perfectas, desmasiados bellas para comer.*

LYNETTE. What did you just say?

BOBBY. (*Translating in his sleep.*) "You are very kind and very beautiful. I wish that I could kiss you and hold your breasts in my hands as if they were perfect fruits, too beautiful to eat."

ESTABAN. *Pon tu mano en mi pecho.*

(LYNETTE looks at ESTABAN.)

BOBBY. (*Still asleep.*) He says to put your hand on his chest. That's as far as you go, Lynette.

LYNETTE. I didn't do anything, Bobby.

ESTABAN. *Escucha a la musica.* (*MUSIC--very soft mixed in with ocean.*) *Esto es lo que está entre los pulsares de corazon despues de todo se va.* (*LYNETTE looks to BOBBY. ESTABAN touches her chin.*) This is what you hear between heart beats after everything else is gone.

(ESTABAN kisses Lynette. HE caresses her face and lays her down on the bed and continues to caress her.
Over this, the ALARM goes off. LIGHTS come up to indicate the morning. BOBBY wakes up, punches the alarm, swears to himself.
LYNETTE starts to sit up as is dragging herself up from her sleep. ESTABAN gently pushes her back down.
BOBBY sits on the edge of the bed, rubbing his face, HE gets up

shuffles to the bathroom.
We hear a garbage truck. ESTABAN starts to leave, LYNETTE
   pulls him back. They continue their embrace over ESTABAN'S
   MUSIC.
We hear the TOILET flush, the MUSIC fades.
ESTABAN starts to get up. LYNETTE tries to pull him back but he
   slips through her hands and disappears LYNETTE wakes up.
FADE OUT.)

THE END

OUT THE WINDOW

by Neal Bell

Out The Window is the co-winner of the Actors Theatre of Louisville 1990 Heideman Award and National Ten-Minute Play Contest.

Out The Window was first produced by the Actors Theatre of Louisville on June 11, 1990. It was directed by Mark Hendren and had the following cast:

JAKE ....Josh Liveright
ANDREA ....Belinda Morgan
Scenic Designer: Paul Owen
Lighting Designer: Jan Thornsberry
Costume Designers: Alan Mosser
Sound Designer: Mark Hendren
Property Master: Mark Bissonnette
Production Manager: Bob Krakower
Stage Manager: Hannah Vesenka
Dramaturg: Carrie Luft

The play subsequently premiered professionally at the Actors Theatre of Louisville on April 6, 1991. It was directed by Bob Krakower and had the following cast:

JAKE ....Tom Stechschulte
ANDY ....Suzanna Hay
Costume Designer: Hollis Jenkins-Evans
Stage Manager: Carey Upton
Dramaturg: Julie Crutcher
Scenic Designer: Paul Owen
Lighting Designer: Karl Haas
Sound Designer: Darron West
Props Master: Ron Riall
Casting NYC: Jay Binder

TIME & PLACE

The action takes place in New York. The time is the present.

OUT THE WINDOW

A kitchen. Early morning LIGHT from the windows over the sink.
Up high, on top of the kitchen table, a wheelchair. In the
wheelchair, JAKE is sprawled, completely out. He's wearing a
wildly disheveled tux. In one dangling hand HE clutches an
empty bottle. JAKE is loudly sawing wood.
The bottle slips from his hand and hits the floor, with a CRASH
that troubles Jake's sleep.

JAKE. (*Eyes closed.*) WHO'S THERE? (*HE reacts to his*
shout.) Oww! Jeez Louise, let me try that again, little softer: Who's
there? Andy ? (*HE feels the surrounding air with his hands.*)
Nothing. Me and my chair.

(Far off a COCK crows.)

JAKE. Hit the snooze-alarm on that rooster, would you? I'm
up. Well, almost up. And I'd open my eyes, to greet the day and
you, but I'm guessing that light would not be what the doctor
ordered, and speaking of tongue and spirit depressors ... One of my
sweat-socks passed away in my mouth, could you bring me a glass
of water, see if I can just flush the sucker, yo, Andrea, hey, little
help ...

(Again the off-stage ROOSTER crows. JAKE winces.)

JAKE. And could somebody kindly get the hook for that bird?

(The ROOSTER crows.)

JAKE. Do I live on a farm? Survey SAYS ... (*HE buzzes*
"no.") OK, did I go to a party so trendy that animal acts were a
part of the entertainment? Survey SAYS ... I don't remember.

Much about that party. At all. I recall a taxi-ride through the Park. And then a mahogany elevator. And then a lot of Republicans. People who *looked* like Republicans, anyway, bow-ties flapping away ... and then you wheeling me out of the madding crowd, and into the dark and onto your bed, *somebody's* bed, whosever bed the party was, and the rest is the kind of history you're condemned to repeat ... which I wouldn't mind, repeating, except next time, Andrea, sweetie, baby, doll, I'd like to remember. The way you feel. The way you taste. The way you move. For both of us. Remember all that, and not black out and be shovelled back into my chair, like a sack of sheep-dip, and shoved out into the hall or wherever I am, stark raving alone, if I *am* alone, if I open my eyes ... if I open my eyes and you've slunk away—Andrea?... I'm going to feel, fair warning here, very crippled up and very done in by Life, as I know it now, and extremely very sorry I ever was born, it is going to get *that* ugly and whiny and borderline-truly-obnoxious, I swear, so be it on your delectable head, if I open my eyes ... (*HE opens his eyes.*) Andrea? (*HE looks around.*) So you slopped me back in my chair after all, and abandoned me halfway up the kitchen ... wall ... (*HE looks down, suddenly realizing his chair is up in the air, on a table.*) ... and screw a Mallard. I'm up on a table. (*Pause.*) Screw a green and yellow Mallard sideways. How'd I ... like a giant entree, defrosting. How'd I get up on a table?

(*ANDY enters, her cocktail dress looking slept-in, toting an almost-empty bottle of booze.*
SHE looks at Jake, in his chair on the table; then SHE squints at her bottle.
Shrugging, SHE polishes off the booze and slumps in a kitchen chair.)

JAKE. Hair of the dog that gummed your ankle?
ANDY. Arf.
JAKE. Little early for that.
ANDY. Go far away. (*Pause.*) I love you.
JAKE. I know.
ANDY. Despite your being high up on a table. By manner of

means unknown. (*Pause.*) And I'm marrying you.

JAKE. I appreciate the condescension.

ANDY. It isn't that. It's a lack of animal cunning—

JAKE. On whose part?

ANDY. Mine. My mother says I must subscribe to survival of the cutest.

JAKE. Your mother thinks I'm cute?

ANDY. I'm on the case. She's half-convinced. She worries about our children.

JAKE. You tell her that automobile collisions aren't passed along in the genes?

ANDY. The carelessness that gets you into them, is.

JAKE. *She* says?...

ANDY. I wonder myself. Get down from there.

JAKE. (*Trying to find an excuse.*) In a minute. The air is clearer.

ANDY. Than what?

(*Offstage, a mournful FOGHORN. JAKE is surprised, and ANDY is bothered.*)

ANDY. And how, of course, would we *have* children?

JAKE. We do it.

ANDY. You never pop.

JAKE. Is that your mother's word? "Pop?"

ANDY. Get DOWN.

JAKE. In what sense?

(*The FOGHORN sounds again, louder.*)

JAKE. I thought I heard a pop. Last night.

ANDY. Champagne. *Cheap* champagne. B-list people. Including us. That kind of party.

JAKE. It was?

(*SHE nods.*)

JAKE. By the sea?

ANDY. No, not by the sea. And not on a farm. Though you babbled on about both, before you went under. A farm with a yard running down to the water. Some place in your head you read about. When you were a kid. Horsies neighing, and moo-cows moo-ing, and lobster lobbing, and foghorns moaning away ...

JAKE. I thought I heard a rooster. A minute ago.

ANDY. Not this high up. On Central Park West. Unless—suppose it's possible—animal sacrifice has trickled down to the horsey-set.

JAKE.—and foghorns.

ANDY. *No.*

JAKE. You heard them too.

ANDY. Get down from there FIVE MINUTES AGO!

(Pause.)

JAKE. I don't know how I got up.

(Pause.)

ANDY. You did it. Congratulations. I'm crying now.

JAKE. Why are you crying?

ANDY. Because you *did* pop. You sorry sodden son-of-a-bitch. You came inside me last night.

JAKE. I didn't.

ANDY. You did. We've been trying for how many months—fifteen? I'd fly, and you thought you would. Ever again. But you did. Last night. You were finally up in the air *with* me. You went off like a Roman candle. And I was the sky you lit up. Way deep inside. But you don't remember.

JAKE. No, wait: maybe I do...

ANDY. You don't. So it never happened. *(Pause.)* It never happened at all. GET OFF OF THIS TABLE! *(Pause.)* How did you get on the table.

JAKE. An awesome wheelie?

(Pause.)

ANDY. You drink too much.

JAKE. And if somebody lit your breath you could spot-weld. Give me a break. And where did *you* sleep last night.

ANDY. In a tub. But I know how I got in the tub. *(Pause.)* Why do you drink so much?

JAKE. I'm afraid.

ANDY. Of what? *(Pause; she suspects the answer.)* Of what?

JAKE. Of you. Of how you think you know me.

ANDY. Oh? Too bad. I *do* know you, pal.

JAKE. And what's the first thing that occurs to you—when you think about me? My sense of rhythm? My brain? My cock? My chair? *(Pause.)* My chair.

ANDY. What chair?

JAKE. Fuck YOU.

ANDY. No: fuck you FIRST.

JAKE. Not *just* a man in a chair. You're smarter than that. But you start with that.

ANDY. I start with just a man—

JAKE. —about whom you know squat—

ANDY. —as do you of the WOMAN, you pushy martyr—

JAKE. A-HA!

ANDY. I worship the ground you roll on, don't give me "A-HA!" Get off of that table you never should have got onto—

JAKE. Why not? I've seen *you* sit on tables before, all devil-may-care—

ANDY. —or I'm walking—

JAKE. Then WALK, for the luvva Mike Wallace, you threaten to walk on me seventeen times a week, at least, and more in months with an "R," so stop sturming and dranging and DO it! WALK.

ANDY. *You* walk!

JAKE. I can't!

ANDY. Then ROLL.

(Pause.)

JAKE. Are you daring me to lay rubber? Step aside ...

(Releasing the brakes on his chair, JAKE starts to push forward. ANDY stops the chair before it can topple over the edge.)

JAKE . Get out of my flight-path, lady.
ANDY. I doubt it severely, bud.
JAKE. You don't get it. Do you? How do you think I landed up here? I flew.
ANDY. I double-dee-doubt it.
JAKE. (*As the truth of it strikes him.*) I flew. Jeez Louise ...
ANDY. Somebody put you up here. As a joke.
JAKE. Who? (*Pause.*) I'm not just a man in a chair.
ANDY. I know.
JAKE. You know that. But you don't know me.
ANDY. I know you didn't fly.
JAKE. Why not?
ANDY. If you could fly ... (*Pause.*) I'm going to find a ladder.

(SHE starts to exit. HE calls after her, stopping her.)

JAKE. "If I could fly ..." (*HE completes her unspoken thought.*) I could do any number of things. Walk, even.
ANDY. Stop.
JAKE. Start *hoping* again I could walk.
ANDY. STOP.
JAKE. Don't you think we should hope any more?
ANDY. I'd rather drink.
JAKE. I never thought I would come.
ANDY. You don't even know if you did.
JAKE. It's coming back. Look out the window.
ANDY. Don't change the subject—
JAKE. I'm not! Look out ...

(ANDY looks out the window and gasps.)

JAKE. We're in an apartment on Central Park West?
ANDY. We were...
JAKE. Can you see the Park?
ANDY. No.
JAKE. Lean out. Can you see the Gulf-and-Western Building?
The Plaza? The street? The horse-and-buggies? Japanese tourists?
Bicycle maniacs? Boom-boxes? Road-apples? Anything?

(Pause.)

ANDY. There's a farm. An old white clapboard farm-house, up
on a rise. And a lawn running down from the house to a rocky
beach. The lawn is steep. It's all wild flowers ...
JAKE. Fog?
ANDY. Yes. But the sun is burning through ... What is it?
JAKE. It isn't a place I read about. It's a place I used to visit.
When I was a kid. Great-Uncle-Somebody's farm. He died a long
time ago, and I never went back ... But I think I was happier there
than I ever have been ...
ANDY. How did we get— ...
JAKE. We flew.

(Pause.)

ANDY. Fly off of the table, then. *(Pause.)* Fly yourself and
your chair back down to the floor. Do it. Now.

(Pause.)

JAKE. I think I've done enough for one day. I'm resting.
ANDY. I have to go. *(SHE starts to exit.)*
JAKE. I remember how we got here.
ANDY. How?
JAKE. You were sitting on me, you were bending over to brush
my face with your hair, and I all of a sudden knew, if you moved
again, I was going to shoot, for the very first time since I hurt
myself, a lot of years in the desert and rain at last, and you started

to move and I grabbed your ass, to hold the moment before I came, I could feel it all about to come down, this wind before a thunderstorm, you were licking my lips, I was holding you still, and holding you still, and just then ... right then ... we were standing beside each other, *standing* holding hands, in this milky light getting lighter, in Great Uncle Somebody's yard ... Uncle *Norbert* ... God, Uncle Norbert ... and we started to run down the hill, that's what we'd do, back then, run down this hill to the water's edge ... and the hill was so steep, you'd hit a place where you knew you couldn't stop anymore, if you tried you'd fall, so you'd just keep running, faster and faster, trying to move your legs as fast as the rest of your body was falling, you'd hear this roar in your ears, and the light on the water would blind your eyes, and all you'd want to do was run on forever.

(Pause.)

ANDY. I had to hope you wouldn't die. And then I had to hope there was still a mind, in this body that hadn't died, and couldn't move. And then, when the mind came back, I had to hope it wasn't buried alive in a body that only lay there, month after month. And then when the body moved at all, the tip of one finger, a twitch, I had to hope it would move again. And that more would move. That your fingers could hold a pencil someday. That your sphincter muscles could hold your piss. That your penis could hold a boner. That you could hold me. So I could love your body! And come. Then I had to hope you could come too.

JAKE. I came.

ANDY. And now you want me to hope that you'll stand on a hill ...

JAKE. I already have. I hope to again. Which I guess is by way of saying that hope is a complicated thing. You give me hope, and I don't know how. *(Pause.)* I also don't know how to get off of this table.

(Pause.)

ANDY. I'll get a ladder ... (*But SHE doesn't move.*)

JAKE. Do you understand what I'm saying? I can never run down that hill again. Except in you.

(ANDY stares at Jake.
Far off a ROOSTER crows, and a FOGHORN sounds.
The LIGHT in the room gets brighter.)

THE END

CONFESSION

A dramatic snapshot

by
Conrad Bishop and Elizabeth Fuller

CHARACTERS

RAYMOND, a man about 40. Salesman.

POLICE DETECTIVE, male about 50.

POLICE STENOGRAPHER, female, 35.

SETTING

A bare room in a mid-western police station. Several chairs and a long narrow table.

CONFESSION

A narrow table. At one end, RAYMOND sits in a wooden chair. He is about forty, in suit and white shirt without a tie, somewhat rumpled. At the opposite end, a female police STENOGRAPHER, focused on her work, writing as the others are speaking. A police DETECTIVE stands by the table, sometimes sitting on the table edge.

RAYMOND speaks in a flat, unemotional tone, but occasionally is unable to continue. The detective is going through a familiar routine.

Long pause. DETECTIVE shifts weight.

RAYMOND. I can't say unless you ask me something.

DETECTIVE. Then what did you do?

RAYMOND. Ok, when we were about to get in the car, I saw another car coming, which I thought looked like it might be stopping, but it didn't. And so we stood there, and when that car had gone I told him to get in the car. And he did, and he didn't struggle. And I started driving off. And he started crying, and down toward 48th I thought about letting him go.

DETECTIVE. But you didn't?

RAYMOND. No.

DETECTIVE. You didn't.

RAYMOND. No.

DETECTIVE. Then what did you do?

RAYMOND. Ok. I ran a red light, and then up a dirt road, over some railroad tracks, turned left over and parked the car over the side of the railroad tracks and I told him get out of the car.

DETECTIVE. The Ford Pinto?

(Pause.)

RAYMOND. There was snow on the ground.

31

STENOGRAPHER. Excuse me. Did he say the Ford Pinto?

DETECTIVE. I said the Ford Pinto. He didn't respond.

RAYMOND. It was the Ford Pinto, yes sir.

STENOGRAPHER. Sorry. I'm new at this.

RAYMOND. That's ok. (*Pause.*) There was snow on the ground. We turned into the woods. I told him stop here, if he did what I told him to, nothing would happen. I told him take off his clothes. Which he did. Then I told him to lay on his back. He didn't want to. So I placed my hands on his shoulders, and indicated with some pressure that he should lay back, but not squeezing.

DETECTIVE. Not squeezing?

RAYMOND. Not squeezing at that time.

(Pause.)

DETECTIVE. Then what did you do?

RAYMOND. Ok, when he had done that, with his back to the ground, not directly on the ground, but on some leaves on the ground in the snow, then this must have been about two o'clock. Because I looked at my watch and I remembered I'd missed lunch. But it was funny because I hadn't, I'd had a BLT and some coffee. And then I knelt on his chest and started to strangle him.

DETECTIVE. Knelt on his chest?

RAYMOND. With my knees.

DETECTIVE. And his back on the ground?

RAYMOND. In the snow. (*Pause.*) Could I take a minute?

DETECTIVE. You need the bathroom?

RAYMOND. No.

DETECTIVE. (*To stenographer.*) Indicate the time. (*Pause.*) Is Larry done? Can he come in and witness?

STENOGRAPHER. He said he'd come in as soon as he could.

DETECTIVE. I don't wanta do this over.

STENOGRAPHER. I don't know. Can't he witness when he signs it?

DETECTIVE. Could you stop with the gum, I got a thing about that.

STENOGRAPHER. Sorry.

RAYMOND. Ok. *(Pause.)* I can't say unless you ask me something.

DETECTIVE. Ok. Then what did you do?

RAYMOND. He struggled and seemed to be in pain, so I stabbed him a couple of times, just not very much, and he just looked rather uncertain. And I just wasn't sure what to do. And he asked me then to go to the hospital, because he was in pain, and then I stabbed him a great many times.

DETECTIVE. Why?

RAYMOND. Just to be sure he was dead. *(Pause.)* I'm having some trouble here right now.

DETECTIVE. Take your time.

(RAYMOND remains sitting, shifting position several times. STENOGRAPHER sits absolutely frozen. DETECTIVE walks around the table, then sits again on the table edge.)

DETECTIVE. *(To stenographer.)* You doing ok? Enjoying your work?

(No response.)

RAYMOND. *(Pulls himself together.)* I can't say unless you ask me something.

DETECTIVE. Did you plan to do this?

RAYMOND. I don't think so. No.

DETECTIVE. You're saying there was no pre-planning involved?

RAYMOND. Not to my knowledge.

DETECTIVE. What did you plan to do?

RAYMOND. I don't know.

DETECTIVE. Why did you do it?

RAYMOND. No reason I can think of. I'm sure there was some reason.

DETECTIVE. Did you at any time fondle, touch privately, play with, do anything personal with this boy?

RAYMOND. Nothing at all.

DETECTIVE. No sexual advances whatsoever of any kind?

RAYMOND. None at all.

DETECTIVE. Have you been at any time ever sexually involved with any males?

RAYMOND. Never.

DETECTIVE. Have you been at any time ever sexually involved with any females?

RAYMOND. Never.

DETECTIVE. Not ever?

RAYMOND. Never.

DETECTIVE. Have you been at any time ever sexually active in any way?

RAYMOND. No. (*Pause.*) Should I talk some more about that, or whatever?

DETECTIVE. I think that's about it for now. (*Vaguely, more or less to stenographer.*) These pathetic sonsabitches. At Comstock they took one of these guys, they shoved a coke bottle up his ass, and then they broke it. Don't ask me how.

STENOGRAPHER. Did you want that in the transcript?

DETECTIVE. Sorry. No offense intended. (*Looks at her pad, then to Raymond.*) Ok honey buns, let's go out and you can wait. We'll get this witnessed, and then we can leave you to play with yourself.

(*RAYMOND gets up, waits. The DETECTIVE goes to door, followed by RAYMOND, then halts. RAYMOND halts. DETECTIVE speaks in a flat tone.*)

DETECTIVE. You know something? I'm talking to you, twinkie-pie. I've got a fifteen-year-old son. You don't know how lucky you are. You don't know how ... fucking ... fucking ... lucky you are.

RAYMOND. I'm sorry.

DETECTIVE. Don't push it.

(*Meanwhile, the STENOGRAPHER has gathered her supplies,*

walked to door, waiting. DETECTIVE starts to open door, looks back. RAYMOND follows. As he passes, the STENOGRAPHER groans. HE halts. SHE grabs him, strikes at him with her pencil, claws at his face, out of control, emitting suppressed moans of rage. RAYMOND covers his face limply. The DETECTIVE, after a moment's surprise, shuts door, intervenes, struggles to bring her under control.)

DETECTIVE. Sally! Stop it! Stop it for Chrissake! *(To Raymond.)* You stand right there, don't move a fucking inch! *(To stenographer.)* Straighten out! Stop! I'm telling you stop! Stop! Stop!

(HE holds her. At last SHE gives up in hysterical exhaustion. HE supports her over to sit in Raymond's chair. RAYMOND stands at a distance. Long silence, except for her sobbing.)

DETECTIVE. Oh Jesus Christ. What the hell. What a terrific day.

STENOGRAPHER. I'm sorry …

DETECTIVE. Anybody give you the information that we have rules, we have procedural rules?

STENOGRAPHER I just …

DETECTIVE. You just shit in your own shoe. I have to report this.

STENOGRAPHER. Doug …

DETECTIVE. I have to report this. Now don't give me any shit. *(To Raymond.)* You have any abrasions?

(RAYMOND removes his hand. His right cheek has a deep gash, bleeding.)

DETECTIVE. Oh Jesus Christ. *(To stenographer.)* What the hell do you think you are doing? You know how long it's gonna take till the chief takes a chance on hiring another bitch? Jesus Christ.

STENOGRAPHER. Doug … I really need this job. I was just

too ...

DETECTIVE. "Oh Doug, I just don't know what came over me!"

STENOGRAPHER. It won't happen ...

DETECTIVE. It sure as hell won't. You're out on your ass.

STENOGRAPHER. Doug, I went to night school for three years—

DETECTIVE. I don't want to hear it—

STENOGRAPHER. I never got a cent of child support, I went through two wage cuts and three lay-offs, and I'd see my little baby's face up to the window watching me go—

DETECTIVE. I don't wanta hear it—

STENOGRAPHER. Doug.

DETECTIVE. Gimme all the excuses. And your husband's a drunk, and he beat you up, and this and that, and your personal needs, and the violence of society, and blah blah blah. Surprise me. You're just pathetic.

STENOGRAPHER. Doug, I really need this job.

RAYMOND. Excuse me ...

(THEY look at him. Long pause.)

RAYMOND. It's all right with me. I don't want her to get in trouble. It's no problem. I'd prefer it if we could just not ... Could we just finish the ...

DETECTIVE. Sally, I'm sorry. It's not an option. They take a look at him, "What happened?" "Oh he had an itch. And scratched it." And then his lawyer gets on it, and very soon we're testifying under oath, and Sally, I need my job too. *(Pause.)* There's no law that says you can't vomit, but you better swallow it back. The job is garbage collecting. You pick it up, cart it off the sidewalk. You don't go crazy and stomp around on the leftovers. That's what they do at the dump. This is a job. We have rules for stuff that leaves marks. *(Opens door.)* Ron, can you come in here a minute?

(Silence. SALLY looks up at Raymond.)

RAYMOND. We have some aspects in common.
STENOGRAPHER. Jesus Christ ...

(SALLY tries to speak, fails. Fade to BLACK.)

THE END

ARIZONA ANNIVERSARIES

by
John Bishop

CHARACTERS

DAVID

SARAH

ANN

ARIZONA ANNIVERSARIES

DAVID, a man in his 30's, enters carrying a suitcase and speaks to the audience.

DAVID. It was my birthday. And since my father died in February, I promised my mother I'd take my vacation in July so I could spend my birthday with her. She lives in Phoenix and from her kitchen window has a view of Camelback Mountain.

(SARAH, his mother, enters.)

DAVID. I think I'll go for a drive.

SARAH. It's a hundred and ten out.

DAVID. The car's air conditioned. I'll go to the mall. Maybe I need a shirt.

SARAH. Take Indian School road to ...

DAVID. I know, Mom. Do you need anything?

SARAH. No. I'm fixing duck.

DAVID. I'm a vegetarian. You know that, Mom. Besides I hate duck.

SARAH. You used to love duck.

DAVID. That was someone else.

SARAH. Some other son? You're a vegetarian?

DAVID. Yes.

SARAH. Then you can eat duck.

DAVID. I'm a strict vegetarian.

SARAH. Relax a little.

DAVID. *(To audience.)* I'm not really a vegetarian but it seemed wrong to eat duck in Arizona. I think you eat duck in Wisconsin. In Arizona you eat ... rattlesnake or something.

(Mall MUSIC.)

41

DAVID. The mall was cool and large. A huge indoor circus of things to buy and want. I tried to think of something I needed. I couldn't. I bought a corn dog. I heard piano music and walked toward it. A woman was playing the piano in piano the store. I was charmed. My Grandmother often told me how, in the 1930's, she used to play piano in Woolworth's ... selling sheet music. The woman was dark and lovely. She glanced at me. (*To her.*) I didn't think they did this anymore.

ANN. Did what?

DAVID. Hire someone to play the piano.

ANN. Hire?

DAVID. The store.

ANN. I'm not hired.

DAVID. You're just ... playing?

ANN. Yes.

DAVID. You're going to buy a piano.

ANN. No.

DAVID. (*To audience with a large grin.*) She just walked in and played one of the pianos. I loved her. (*To her.*) May I buy you an Orange Julius?

(*THEY sit with paper cups.*)

DAVID. (*To audience.*) She was handsome. Earnest. With a dark shadow in back of her eyes. (*To her.*) I don't usually talk to strange women in malls.

ANN. You don't?

DAVID. My mother and grandmother play the piano.

ANN. My father played.

DAVID. I had to get out of the house. And it's too hot to walk. Except in a mall. It's my birthday.

ANN. It's my wedding anniversary. Nine years.

DAVID. Hey! Congratulations.

ANN. We met here.

DAVID. The mall.

ANN. Cineplex Eight. Standing in line.

DAVID. So you came to celebrate ...

ANN. Remember.

DAVID. ... the anniversary.

ANN. The meeting.

DAVID. Do you live in Phoenix?

ANN. I live in Bakersfield. Which is in California.

DAVID. And what are you doing in Phoenix? Vacation?

ANN. My father died.

DAVID. I'm sorry.

ANN. I'm here to sell the house. And furnishings. Have you ever held a yard sale?

DAVID. No.

ANN. I'm told that's the easiest way. Sell everything. I'm inclined to just give it away. I don't want to haggle over money.

DAVID. Your mother is dead.

ANN. Yes.

DAVID. Is there much of value?

ANN. I don't know. Doubtful. He worked for the city.

DAVID. My father also died.

ANN. They do that.

DAVID. So I came here to ... my mother wanted me to spend my birthday with her.

ANN. Are you married? No, of course not, or you wouldn't be here on your birthday.

DAVID. I guess not.

ANN. I'm divorced.

DAVID. Oh? I thought ... you were here ... the anniversary ...

ANN. Of the meeting. It was the best part.

DAVID. I'm sorry.

(SHE shrugs.)

DAVID. I have this feeling. As I sit here talking to you. That I know you. Have talked to you before.

ANN. I don't think so.

DAVID. You don't feel that?

ANN. Well ... you are easy to talk to but ...

DAVID. See?

ANN. (*Laughs.*) But, I don't remember ever meeting you.

DAVID. Another century, maybe.

ANN. Is this a line?

DAVID. It's a feeling.

ANN. I don't believe in that sort of thing anymore. I did. When I was little. My father read books to me. He was fascinated by metaphysics ... reincarnation ... that.

DAVID. Anything's possible.

ANN. If that were so ... if life somehow goes on ... my father would have let me know ... sent a message. He was ... he had that gift.

DAVID. What gift?

ANN. He knew things others didn't know. Before they knew them ... he knew. He said it was because he was tuned in.

DAVID. To people?

ANN. To some kind of ongoing, universal flow.

DAVID. He was spiritual.

ANN. He thought he was.

DAVID. What kind of message would he have sent you?

ANN. "Hold on. It gets better." (*SHE smiles.*)

DAVID. (*To audience.*) She has a beautiful smile. It begins in her eyes and sort of creeps down to her lips. I watched it till it faded as she drank the last of her Orange Julius.

ANN. I have to go.

DAVID. Can I give you a lift?

ANN. Where are you from?

DAVID. New York City.

ANN. Well, people don't walk to malls in Arizona in July. I have a car. (*SHE starts to go.*)

DAVID. I was planning on driving to the Chiricahua mountains and Cochise's stronghold. I'm interested in Indian history. But I don't have to. I'd like to take you to dinner. Celebrate our anniversaries. And I could help you with the yard sale. I've never done it but I'm probably good at that sort of thing.

ANN. Well ... if you want to.

(*SHE exits. SARAH enters.*)

SARAH. I hope you like the duck. I cooked it with a lot of vegetables.

DAVID. Mom, do you know how to hold a yard sale?

SARAH. Who died?

DAVID. A friend of mine's father.

SARAH. We don't have yard sales in Arizona. Too hot. (*Beat.*) Put up signs all over the neighborhood. Arrows pointing the way. Shouldn't look too professional. Use crayon. Put everything for sale in the garage and one room. Don't use the toilet after they've gone.

DAVID. (*To audience.*) I took her to dinner. Mexican.

ANN. You haven't asked what I do for a living.

DAVID. Haven't got around to it.

ANN. I'm a broker.

DAVID. Okay. (*Beat.*) You haven't asked what I do.

ANN. You're a lawyer.

DAVID. No.

ANN. You're a doctor.

DAVID. Yes.

ANN. What kind?

DAVID. Sports medicine.

ANN. Feet.

DAVID. Mostly knees.

ANN. I jog.

DAVID. Good.

ANN. Any advice?

DAVID. Keep doing it.

ANN. I like to feel strong. You look strong. Are you an athlete?

DAVID. I backpack.

ANN. Climb mountains?

DAVID. Sometimes.

ANN. Because they're there?

DAVID. Because it would take too long to go around them.

ANN. Sleep in the woods? Near a lake.

DAVID. Upon occasion. Listen to the loons. Ever hear a loon?

ANN. No.

(HE imitates a loon.)

ANN. That should get a waiter.

DAVID. *(To audience.)* Next day we drove to Sedona.

ANN. It was not that long ago that people came to Arizona for the air. Now it is dangerous. From the exhausts of all the cars.

DAVID. Of all the people coming here for the air.

ANN. We have fucked everything up.

DAVID. We? I haven't.

ANN. But that's the way of things, isn't it? What begins ... ends. So you have to ask yourself ... why begin?

DAVID. That's exactly what you must never ask yourself.

ANN. Beginnings are wonderful. Filled with promise. Endings are horrible.

DAVID. It's a matched pair. A package deal. Buy one, get one free. *(To audience.)* That night we went back to her father's house, a small ranch house, and made love. Afterward I fell asleep. When I awakened I heard her in the kitchen.

ANN. *(Offering him a can of soda.)* I was thirsty. Pepsi?

DAVID. *(Takes a sip.)* I thought we were amazing. *(Beat.)* I don't do this often.

ANN. You don't have to say that.

DAVID. But I don't. You don't either.

ANN. No.

DAVID. You were so ... eager. And so shy. And so beautiful.

ANN. You felt ... very good to me.

DAVID. *(To audience.)* I arranged the sale for her. Put out signs. Piled the stuff in the garage and living room. Took their money. She sat in the dining room in a broken canvas lawn chair. Toward evening, while people were still browsing, she got in her car and drove away. By 10:30 the house was bare, except for junk no one wanted. I sat down on the floor and waited for her. At midnight I left the money in an envelope on the mantle. And the next day, on my way to the Chiricahuas, I drove by the house. But she was gone. The money and her luggage also. I parked in a campground and hiked to the high country where Cochise had lived. I wondered what he would think if I drove him to a shopping mall. He probably wouldn't find anything he needed either. I spent a week in the mountains. The nights were cool and clear and I sat by my tent and thought about how much I liked her. And the way we fit ... she and I. It was remarkable. At the end of the week, I drove back to Phoenix and ate duck salad with Mom and caught a plane home.

(SARAH hands him his suitcase. HE kisses her goodbye.)

DAVID. I think sometimes of the anniversaries we celebrated together. And how disappointed she was with life. And that probably her father's death was just one more disappointment. And then I think about the fact that he believed he was spiritual and her greater disappointment that he never sent her a message. And I recall my aimless trip to the mall that day. And I wonder if maybe he did. She just didn't get it. (*HE carries his bag offstage.*)

THE END

MENTAL RESERVATION

by
Roger Cornish

CHARACTERS

HE

SHE

TIME & PLACE

MENTAL RESERVATION

AT RISE, THEY are drinking coffee.

SHE. No I didn't.

HE. Yes you did. I asked you if I was going bald, and you said "no." (*Bending his head and tapping the thin spot.*) Look at that!

SHE. You can't even see there.

HE. The ceiling of my elevator is a mirror, so I can see there. And what I see is skin.

SHE. OK. If you knew the answer, why did you ask?

HE. Maybe so you'd lie.

SHE. Well, so I did.

HE. But if you were really my friend, you wouldn't lie to me.

SHE. Aaaaaaaagh! (*SHE cuts her throat with her coffee spoon.*) You drive a person crazy.

HE. It's true. It doesn't matter what I *wanted*, your friend doesn't lie to you.

SHE. I didn't lie. I made a mental reservation.

HE. A what?

SHE. A mental reservation. When I said "no, you're not going bald," I was thinking in comparison with Telly Savalas and the late Yul Bryner.

HE. And that makes it not a lie?

SHE. Ethically speaking.

HE. *Ethically*!

SHE. Read *Medical Ethics*.

HE. What, the oxymoron book?

SHE. Read it. Suppose your patient has a temp of a hundred and three and he asks you how his temp is. You don't want to worry him, he's *dying*, right? So you say "your temp is normal today."

HE. That's not a lie?

SHE. No, because in your head you're thinking "normal for

51

somebody that's going to be dead tomorrow." See, there's no deceit in your *mind*. If he doesn't figure out that "normal today" can mean a lot of things, it's not your fault. And you've acted in your patient's best interests.

HE. So you told me I wasn't going bald because you were thinking I'd be dead tomorrow and I still have a lot of hair under the circumstances.

SHE. I didn't want you to feel bad—I'm your friend.

HE. Mental reservation.

SHE. Yep.

HE. So nobody ever has to tell the truth.

SHE. Oh well ...

HE. *Never.* I betcha I don't *ever* have to tell you the truth.

SHE. (*Laughing.*) Well, if you don't, I don't.

HE. I betcha.

SHE. How much you wanna bet?

HE. I betcha my Yugo.

SHE. You don't have a Yugo.

HE. Mental reservation: I'm thinking "in the event when I'm finally a wealthy physician, I'm the first to buy a Yugo instead of a Mercedes."

SHE. I think he's got it!

HE. What do *you* wanna bet?

SHE. Betcha my virginity.

HE. You don't *have* your virginity.

SHE. Mental reservation: "Which I will try to get back from the guy I gave it to in the twelfth grade."

HE. Did you cheat on the Anatomy final?

SHE. Yes.

HE. Now I know that's a lie.

SHE. In the sense that I brought in my fingers (*Counting on her fingers.*) to use as a memory aid.

HE. Weak, weak!

SHE. Have I gained weight?

HE. No.

SHE. You are sweet but a liar.

HE. Not in comparison to Roseanne Barr.

SHE. Rat! What specialty do you plan to pursue?

HE. Proctology.

SHE. Aaack, puke, bleagh!

HE. If pediatrics, psychiatry, dermatology, cardiology, and gynecology are all closed. What about you?

SHE. Obstetrics.

HE. Naaaahh ...

SHE. If they'll sell me liability insurance for a dollar a year.

HE. This game's starting to make sense. (*After a sip of coffee.*) Should a physician marry another physician?

SHE. Certainly.

HE. Really?

SHE. Of course. With the mental reservation that the physician she marries helps get their practice started by converting to nurse/receptionist.

HE. Ow! Women's lib is ugly.

SHE. Are you my best friend?

HE. I'm afraid not.

SHE. (*Forgetting the game.*) Oh, Billy, that hurts.

HE. A man's best friend is his dog. You can only be my second best friend.

SHE. Oh, well, that's OK.

HE. (*Beat.*) Did you go out with Farmer last night?

SHE. Nope.

(*HE sits back and folds his arms.*)

SHE. When you consider that we *met* in the parking lot and went *into* a restaurant.

HE. Uh huh.

SHE. (*Beat.*) Do you think I'm attractive?

HE. (*Beat.*) No.

SHE. No? Oh, that's good—that's a lie, right?

HE. No.

SHE. It isn't? Oh, it's not a lie, meaning yes, it is a lie, because you found a tricky mental reservation, right? (*Instantly.*) Don't say anything—I'm not asking a question!

HE. Did Farmer come on to you last night?

SHE. ... No.

HE. That's a lie anytime. I know Farmer.

SHE. He came *on* to me months ago, so there was no coming on left to do. I don't like this game anymore, do you?

HE. No.

SHE. Good. Or do you—is that the truth?

HE. Mental reservation: I've just started to like it, so "any more" isn't applicable. Did you sleep with Farmer last night?

SHE. No—I mean yes.

HE. Yes?

SHE. Yes for no. So yes.

HE. Mental reservation?

SHE. I uh slept with Farmer if uh, if you consider the fact that at one-thirty A.M., when I went to sleep, about a million other people in this city were asleep, probably including Farmer, so I was uh, sleeping with Farmer—and all those other people.

HE. With the mental reservation that you were sleeping with those other people together in the same city, but that you were sleeping with Farmer in the same bed?

SHE. No, that's not what I meant. I meant I slept with Farmer in that ... no, just plain no, I didn't sleep with Farmer. Period.

HE. With the reservation that you were both too busy having sex to sleep?

SHE. Yes!

HE. Ah.

SHE. No, yes for no! I'm lying—no, I quit—game over!

HE. You mean it?

SHE. Yes, plain yes. We'll just tell the regular truth from now on, all right?

HE. Yes.

SHE. Do you *mean* it?

HE. Yes.

SHE. Stop that, please.

HE. All right.

SHE. Is that why you're angry with me—Farmer?

HE. No.

SHE. It *is* Farmer. You think I'm cheap?

HE. No.

SHE. Please, let's quit—I can't do this anymore. (*Pause.*) I don't care about Farmer. Farmer's just ... you know me—I'm a trollop. Why do you care about Farmer?

HE. I don't.

SHE. ... Meaning you don't care about *Farmer* as Farmer, only what I do with him. (*Pause.*) What do you want me to say?

HE. Nothing.

SHE. Meaning something.

HE. Nothing if I have to tell you what to say.

SHE. Something. What? (*Beat.*) That I love you?

HE. No.

SHE. That I *do.*

HE. (*Beat.*) Do you?

SHE. Yes.

HE. Yes?

SHE. Yes with mental reservation: considering that love implies the good feelings any person should feel for a friend and not something else that's just ... what people do sometimes.

(*HE finishes his coffee.*)

SHE. Do you love me?

HE. ... No.

SHE. Meaning yes, except for a mental reservation ...

HE. (*Rising.*) No. (*HE exits.*)

BLACKOUT

THE END

AFTER YOU

by
Steven Dietz

After You was first produced at the Actors Theatre of Louisville on December 10, 1990. It was directed by Bob Krakower and had the following cast:

AMY ....Kristen Harris

BEN...Tony Ward

Scenic Design: Paul Owen
Lighting Designer: Casey Clark
Costume Designer: Kevin McLeod
Sound Designer: Darron West
Property Master: Mark Bissonnette
Production Manager: Bob Krakower
Stage Manager: John David Flak
Dramaturg: Emily F. Morse

CHARACTERS

AMY, a woman in her early thirties.

BEN, a man in his early thirties.

TIME & PLACE

The present.
A chair in a room in an American city.

A song to be used as a possible musical frame around the play is Bob Dylan's "Most of the Time" from the album *Oh Mercy* (CBS Records, 1989), however, producers of this play are hereby CAUTIONED that permission to produce this play does not include rights to use this song in production. Producers should contact the copyright owners directly for rights.

AFTER YOU

AMY sits in a simple wooden chair. She wears a white cotton robe.
On the ground in front of her is a basin of hot water, a mug of
    shaving creme, and a straight razor.
Nearby, a single white candle burns.
BEN stands near Amy. He wears jeans, boots and a white t-shirt.
    He has a white towel draped over his shoulder.
THEY stare at each other for a long time.

    AMY. I'm cold.
    BEN. You'll be fine.
    AMY. Ben, I'm—
    BEN. You'll put your feet in, and it'll—watch, I'll show you—

(AMY sits in the chair.)

    BEN. There, now put your—
    AMY. (*Having put one foot in the water.*) Aaaaauuuuuggggghhhhh.
    BEN. That's good, right?
    AMY. It's—
    BEN. Other foot.

(SHE puts her other foot in, stifling her impulse to scream.)

    BEN. Right? That's good. (*HE applies shaving creme to her*
legs after warming them with a wet towel.*)
    AMY. Ben?
    BEN. Hmm?
    AMY. To what do I owe this?
    BEN. It was a thought I had.

(Silence.)

BEN. You want me to go?

AMY. No.

BEN. This would have been one of my regrets.

AMY. You have a list?

BEN. You have a problem with that?

AMY. Just fishing.

(Silence.)

BEN. I always wanted to do this. Fair?

AMY. *(Stares at him.)* Fair.

(Silence.)

BEN. Bend.

(SHE bends her leg as he shaves a bit.)

BEN. Yes. It's on the list. I don't leave things—do I? You know this. I don't—

AMY. It's an obligation.

BEN. I didn't—

AMY. That's you to the quick. See it through to the—dot the i's, cross the t's, no matter what, no matter the carnage, no matter if the getting there is fruitless or wrenching or—

BEN. Do you want this or not?

(Silence.)

AMY. Ben.

BEN. Fruitless?

AMY. Look.

BEN. Wrenching? *Please.*

AMY. Ben, wait—

BEN. I don't need to do this. I don't have this—there is not this *thing* welling up in me that says *do this*, okay? I don't need to do this, Amy. I really don't.

AMY. Fuck you.

(Silence.)

BEN. Say again?
AMY. You heard me.
BEN. Yes.

(Silence.)

AMY. (*Smiles a bit.*) Yes?
BEN. Yes. (*HE begins to shave her legs.*)
AMY. I shaved you once. Do you remember?
BEN. I'd forgotten that.
AMY. Are you paying me back?

(BEN starts wiping some of the creme off her legs.)

AMY. Ben —
BEN. I'm remembering now.
AMY. What are you doing?
BEN. I'm taking the creme off your legs. I'm shaving you without the creme.
AMY. Why?
BEN. I am paying you back.
AMY. How was I to know your face was that sensitive?
BEN. Maybe the blood.
AMY. What're you—ouch, careful.
BEN. Maybe the blood should have been a warning.
AMY. Right.
BEN. A sign. Blood is a sign. Watch blood.
AMY. It was harder than I thought. It looked so easy every morning when you did it.
BEN. Straighten.

(SHE straightens her leg, HE reapplies the creme.)

BEN. Thank you.

AMY. The slope of it, you know, the landscape—

BEN. You thought you knew my face.

AMY. I thought I knew your face.

(SHE is touching his face. HE takes her hand away, gently, and continues shaving her.)

AMY. Do you have these written down?

BEN. These—

AMY. These things. This list of obligations. You what, over time you go home and check them off? Then one day you're done owing me? One day I'm a clean slate.

BEN. This is shit you found charming, this is—

AMY. I never found—

BEN. What, now you—

AMY. I never found that charming. I never did.

BEN. Be bigger, Amy. Be bigger than that. Admit that my—

AMY. Your *what*?

BEN. My scrupulousness—

AMY. Ha.

BEN. That my sense of detail, my noting and crossing off of tasks was a charming thing to you. A thing you used to call *concern*. And a thing that you have since *re-named*, a thing you now—

AMY. Manipulation.

BEN. See, yes, now you have re-named it. And, no, I don't have them written down. I can stop, okay? I don't need to do this. I wanted to see you, but if you'd rather pretend that each other is dead or something, then—

AMY. Ben. It's me. Save breath. I know you know how this is. You missed a spot. I know you know this is nice.

(Silence. HE shaves her.)

BEN. You in love?

AMY. Have you been waiting to hold a razor to me and ask me

that?

BEN. I don't miss your sarcasm.

AMY. You might.

BEN. It's been a year. I don't.

AMY. You will.

BEN. I might.

AMY. No.

BEN. You're not?

AMY. I'm not.

BEN. C'mon. Nobody?

AMY. I didn't know we'd be graded on this.

BEN. I'd like to be.

AMY. In love.

BEN. Yes. I'd like to know who's after you. I'd like to have that settled.

AMY. Is there a line forming?

BEN. I definitely won't.

AMY. What?

BEN. Miss your sarcasm. Hold still.

AMY. Don't begrudge me my jealously. I like my jealously. It keeps me close to you.

BEN. I'll tell you about jealousy: I resent people who encounter you. Check-out clerks you hand money to. Waiters who bring your wine and french fries. Strangers who share your elevator and ride to your floor though it's five floors out of their way.

AMY. You're the only one who ever did that.

BEN. I resent Jehovah's Witnesses who come to your door. They get you without caution. They get you straight ahead.

AMY. And you get?

BEN. I get judgment and longing.

AMY. Well, that's what's left.

BEN. I don't believe that. (*Silence. HE shaves her.*) We were at a dinner party for one of your publishers, we didn't really know anyone there. Do you remember this?

AMY. When?

BEN. A year ago.

AMY. Keep going.

BEN. We sat at opposite ends of the table, not saying a word, and a man that neither of us knew looked at us, and said: You two must have a delicious secret.

(He looks at her. Silence.)

AMY. I remember.
BEN. You got shy.
AMY. Yes.
BEN. It looked good on you.
AMY. I've been trying to remember the last moment when it was still lovely. I think maybe that was it.
BEN. It didn't change in a moment, Amy. It didn't all—
AMY. Of course not. I'm just saying there was a point (I believe this, I do), there was a point when it began to *turn*. A point before the screaming and the lies. Before counseling and jealousy and dividing up our friends. And the moment before that point was still innocent, still lovely. At that moment we still wanted to show each other off.

(HE wipes her legs with a wet towel. SHE touches his hair, pulls him closer to her. THEY kiss. THEY part.)

BEN. Who's after me?
AMY. Someone ... reminiscent.
BEN. Of what?
AMY. Of who I thought you were. Fair?
BEN. Fair.
AMY. And ditto I would guess?
BEN. Ditto.
AMY. It's all misdirection and faulty theories. All we really want is to find someone we are certain to dazzle.

(Silence. HE closes her robe, covering her legs.)

BEN. This completes our mission.
AMY. Stay for a glass of wine.

BEN. You replaced the glasses we broke?

AMY. It's been a year.

BEN. Thanks.

AMY. But?

BEN. I'd love to.

AMY. What, you've got a date.

BEN. Yes. Jealous?

AMY. Fuck you.

BEN. Good.

AMY. Where are you—wait, *may I?* Where are you going on this date?

BEN. My house.

AMY. Brazen of you.

BEN. I thought so.

AMY. And who is—wait, *may I?* Who is the lucky victim?

BEN. A three-hundred pound blind piano tuner named Delmore. I've been trying to get this piano tuned for a year. He'll be at my house at six. Sorry.

AMY. You have a piano now?

BEN. Yes.

AMY. Pets?

BEN. Fish.

AMY. Fish?

BEN. I'm working up to pets. How 'bout a raincheck?

AMY. Hmm?

BEN. On the drink.

AMY. That's you to the quick. I'll let you know. Fair?

BEN. Yes.

AMY. Okay.

BEN. Great word, fair.

(HE puts on a jacket, prepares to leave. Long silence.)

BEN. Be well.

AMY. Thank you. I'd like to see your piano. Some month or other.

BEN. I don't have a piano. You know that.

AMY. I know that.

(Silence.)

AMY. Ben?
BEN. Hmm?
AMY. There's blood on my leg.
BEN. Watch blood. Blood is a sign.

(BEN looks at her for a moment, then exits. AMY sits in the chair and begins rubbing lotion on her legs as the LIGHTS slowly fade to BLACK.)

THE END

PYRAMID EFFECT

by
Marcia Dixcy

Pyramid Effect premiered at the Actors Theatre of Louisville on December 14, 1987. It was directed by Bob Krakower. The cast was:

BUD ....Del Pentecost
STEVE..Al Proia
ROBBIE...Rob Campbell
MEGAN ....Kate Fleming
ELAINE ....Adrianne Krstansky
LULIE ....Heidi Swedberg

Set Design: Robert T. Odorisio
Costume Design: Susan Snowden
Lighting Designers: Lynn Lefkoff and Michael Milkovich
Sound Design: Mark Hendren
Property Master: Ron Riall
Production Managers: Bob Krakower and Chris Wineman
Production Stage Manager: Veronica Pullins-Bishop
Dramaturg: Jon Jory

CHARACTERS
(All college-aged)

BUD—Large, congenial, some Texas accent.
STEVE—Was an Indiana high school basketball champ.
ROBBIE—Overcompensates for his inadequacies.
MEGAN—Practical, open-minded, slightly acerbic.
ELAINE—Mellow—has benefitted from yoga.
LULIE—Scampish, very agile. Enjoys herself.

PYRAMID EFFECT

The play starts in BLACKOUT.

ROBBIE. No, not there. Jeez, are you crazy?! Move your knee … No, ow! … Not in the middle of my back.

LULIE. Sorry, hon. I thought that was your shoulder there. (*Giggles.*) Wait. Wait. *Wait*! I gotta rest a minute.

ROBBIE. No, there's no way. Get on top or I'm gonna lose it.

ELAINE. You're just wasting energy, Robbie. Take deep breaths. Breeeeeathe in. Breeeeeathe out. Breeeeeathe. Breeeeeathe in, Ak! Lulie, watch your nails. No, no, nooooooooo.

(LIGHTS come up slowly on a human pyramid. THREE MALES at the base. L to R: BUD, STEVE and ROBBIE. TWO FEMALES on the middle layer: MEGAN, ELAINE. LULIE has just reached the top.)

LULIE. That's it. Zingo! We're here; we're set. Do you believe it?!

(Leans down to hug the necks of MEGAN and ELAINE. MEGAN and ELAINE speak on top of one another.)

MEGAN. Your knee is squashing my lumbar vertebrae!

ELAINE. No please! You're twisting my neck wrong.

ROBBIE. Stabilize!

STEVE. (*Head turned to Robbie.*) Yo Robbie, our air traffic controller.

(MEGAN, ELAINE and ROBBIE speak on top of each other.)

MEGAN. All right, that's better, that's better. Keep your knee right there where I've packed my sweats with Kotex.

69

ELAINE. (*To Robbie and Steve.*) Don't you two start, I can't hold up over a lot of negativity!

ROBBIE. (*To Steve.*) I think somebody better exert some control or we won't stay up four minutes—let alone four hours.

(*LULIE has been back on her haunches straddling MEGAN and ELAINE. SHE's taken out some suntan lotion from a shoulder bag and is smoothing it over her arms.*)

LULIE. Great view guys! This is a *great* view!

BUD. (*The largest, most stalwart of the group.*) Did you say four hours?

MEGAN. Yeh, Bud. Where've you been? What do you think we're doing?

BUD. Fred told me two. Two to break the record.

LULIE. Boy! Fred better have this straight, 'cause way down there two hours means a lot more than it does up here. (*SHE peers way down.*)

ROBBIE. Two hours for the University record. Four hours, three minutes twenty-nine seconds for *the* record, the Guinness Record. The record that wins us Target's $2,500 Challenge.

STEVE. Is that before or after taxes?

MEGAN. And is it split how? Evenly because of the danger and anxiety on the top versus the weight on the bottom. Or is it ...

BUD. (*Calling down.*) Fred, you bimbo! Can you hear me down there?

LULIE. Bud?

MEGAN. This is no time to be unkind to those below you, Bud.

BUD. (*Still calling down.*) You pain in the patootee. Got me here on a wicked hangover.

ELAINE. Calm down, Bud. We all have needs here. Take it one hour at a time. Brea ...

ROBBIE. Elaine, dear, even Bud may have better things to do with his mind than concentrate on his breathing. Breathing is something even the lowest forms of life can do without benefit of intelligent thought.

(BUD starts a small hiccup.)

STEVE. *(To Bud.)* C'mon, guy. You can use two hundred bucks. Think ahead.

LULIE. And, Bud, think of my career, and the coverage that only four hours can bring.

(BUD hiccups again, slightly stronger.)

STEVE. Hey, four hours is no sweat, Lulie.

MEGAN. *(To Lulie.)* And you got yourself in a position that cries out for telephoto lenses.

LULIE. God, I hope so.

BUD. I don't know ... HICCUP.

ROBBIE. *(To Lulie.)* So it was Fred's concern for your modeling career that convinced him to place you up there Lulie?

ELAINE. *(Sincerely.)* That was nice.

MEGAN. *(To Bud.)* What's going on. Are you spazing out or what's happening?

LULIE. *(Peers down from above.)* Bud?

(BUD hiccups again. MEGAN, ELAINE and LULIE move up and down slightly.)

STEVE. Cut it out, Megan. Stop bouncing my butt.

MEGAN. I'm not; it's Bud.

ROBBIE. *(To Steve.)* Bud is bouncing your butt?

BUD. *(Hiccupping loudly.)* I've got the hiccups. I've got the dang blasted hiccups!

MEGAN. Great! You just made me bite my tongue.

ELAINE. He just got too upset. Hiccups are simply a stress reaction.

MEGAN. Gross, my tongue is bleeding, oh gross.

ROBBIE. Stress reaction! What you're hearing are the dying bellows of two six-packs of Moosehead.

(Loud HICCUP and COMMOTION.)

ROBBIE. Down Bullwinkle, steady, boy.

STEVE. Chill out, Robbie. You're giving me an earache.

MEGAN. I'm serious guys. This is like a hemorrhage. In a minute I'm gonna be choking.

ELAINE. You need to apply pressure to stop the bleeding. Do you have a Kleenex or something?

LULIE. (*Pulls scarf from around head.*) Here, take my bandana. (*Leans over to let Megan grab it in her mouth.*)

ROBBIE. Yes, Elaine, why don't you make a tourniquet?

(Loud HICCUP. MEGAN screams muffled by scarf.)

LULIE. I think we oughta do something hiccup-wise.

STEVE. Don't worry Lulie.

ELAINE. Well, it's muscle relaxation, really. His esophagus is going into traumatic spasms.

STEVE. Ya know, I think I did read about that somewhere ... some guy who had hiccups for eight years! They tried ...

ROBBIE. Oh sure. Is this helping to relax you over there Bud?

(Loud HICCUP.)

ELAINE. (*Just barely hanging on.*) Perhaps if he tried holding his breath ...

(MEGAN makes muffled sounds of agreement.)

ROBBIE. I thought you just said *taking* a breath was supposed to be so relaxing.

ELAINE. Well ...

LULIE. Cut it out, Robbie. Holding your breath is a valid cure for hiccups. Anyone knows that.

(Loud HICCUP. More muffled SOUNDS from MEGAN.)

STEVE. Yeh. This guy with the hiccups for eight years? They

held him under water in one of those backyard swimming pools?
Something like five minutes. The hiccups just kept rising to the
surface.

*(Loud HICCUP prompting MEGAN to spit out scarf in an
outburst.)*

MEGAN. Shut up and let him hold his breath before I get really
nauseous!
LULIE. OK, Bud, get ready, big breath: one, two, three ...

*(BUD heaves a massive breath, almost toppling all above ...
several beats of silence.)*

ELAINE. Lulie could you move that knee back about two
inches?
MEGAN. There's no way we're going to keep this up four
hours, no way. How long have we been up here already?
ROBBIE. I don't know. Steve, turn your wrist around so I can
see your watch.
LULIE. *(Showing her jazzy Swatch to Megan.)* Here, I've got it.
MEGAN. How am I supposed to read that? They're no
numbers. They're no hands are there? Are they those little
lightning bolts?
LULIE. *(Cupping her hand over her watch face.)* Yeh, they
glow in the dark ... it's ... ah ...
ROBBIE. *(Finally reading Steve's watch.)* Two fourteen.
LULIE. I say twenty after.
MEGAN. So how much longer?
ROBBIE. Three hours, fifty-four minutes.

(Large subterranean HICCUP.)

MEGAN. *(Swaying.)* Not of this there won't be.
ELAINE. Just keep holding on, Bud. Just hold right through the
hiccup.
STEVE. You know what finally stopped 'em? His wife fired a

gun point blank, right at his face. I mean it was empty but it scared
him so bad it finally stopped 'em.

(BUD glares over at Steve, face beet red.)

   LULIE. Hey, Bud, how's it going?

(BUD begins quivering.)

   STEVE. But after that, they got divorced. It was just ...
   MEGAN. Are we going to follow this man to his grave?

*(BUD now vibrating the whole group, starts to let air squeak out
   like a trumpet.)*

   ELAINE. I think you better release now, Bud. Just let the air
out slowly.
   MEGAN. Yeh, we're liable to go out like the Hindenburg.
   ROBBIE. *(Looking down to folks below.)* OK, OK, hang on
down there. We're experiencing technical difficulties.

*(BUD lets all his air out with a large lurch ... silence for a few
   beats.)*

   STEVE. You feeling better now guy?
   LULIE. Bud?
   ELAINE. Give him space.
   ROBBIE. Oh fine.

(Small HICCUP from BUD.)

   ROBBIE. Was that you again, Bud?
   MEGAN. I think I just felt my two hundred dollars heave it's
dying breath.
   LULIE. What about water? What about the thing of drinking
water upside-down?
   MEGAN. That ought to be a cinch.

LULIE. (*Smacking top of head with joy.*) I've got my thermos! (*Reaching into bag.*)

ROBBIE. Did you consider there might be a minimum baggage allotment on this venture, Lulie?

LULIE. Here, Bud. Here's some V-8.

ELAINE. (*Perking up.*) Oh, can I have a sip?

BUD. Give me a break. (*Large HICCUP.*)

MEGAN. (*Taking control.*) No! Now you take this and try to drink it upside down.

(*MEGAN takes cup from Lulie and bends down to reach Bud's mouth.*)

BUD. I can't drink V-8 juice right side up.

(*LULIE pours another Dixie-cup for Elaine.*)

MEGAN. Well, this is important, so you got to try. Lulie, move from my shoulder a sec so I can get this cup under his mouth backwards. (*Contortions trying to execute this maneuver.*)

STEVE. OK, Buddy. This glass of V-8 is your ticket to fame and fortune.

BUD. Mmmm, hurrah, gurgh, cough, cough ...

STEVE. Steady.

MEGAN. Don't spill it, Bud.

BUD. Hnah, phah! It went up my nose!

ELAINE. You ought to watch out. He could actually become asphyxiated that way.

ROBBIE. Fine, as long as it cures his hiccups.

(*Spastic painful HICCUP from BUD.*)

STEVE. Bummer.

MEGAN. Now I'm starting to feel really discouraged.

LULIE. C'mon Megan!

ELAINE. I've heard about breathing into a paper bag. That way the carbon dioxide accumulates and the body thinks it's kind of an emergency situation, so the whole digestive system just shuts down.

ROBBIE. And do the hiccups stop or are you sharing a form of dietetic breathing?

(Another LARGE HICCUP.)

ROBBIE. Lulie, we're now waiting for the bag.

LULIE. *(Looking furiously through her stuff.)* Darn! I had my Oreos in a kind of a ... I don't know, they must be back on the counter ... but ... I thought it was a balloon.

MEGAN. What?

LULIE. A balloon. You blow up a balloon for hiccups.

MEGAN. Do you have a balloon?

LULIE. 'Course not. Why would I bring a balloon with me?

BUD. I *(Large HICCUP.)* don't want a balloon.

ROBBIE. But you do want two hundred dollars. And it's not just your two hundred dollars you're hiccupping away; it's two thousand, three hundred belonging to your friends. Friends who need it.

ELAINE. Putting pressure on him will only make them worse.

STEVE. Ah, I might have it. *(Tries to reach for his left shirt pocket but can't maintain balance.)*

MEGAN. Watch it, Steve.

LULIE. Whoa!

STEVE. OK, listen, one of you has to reach inside my left shirt pocket.

MEGAN. Yeh ... and what?

STEVE. Just do it.

MEGAN. All right, all right. Lulie can you move over to Elaine for a minute?

*(LULIE does s   qo—much unsteady hanging on. HICCUP from
    BUD.)*

ELAINE. Lulie your knee, no your knee has got to go ... uh ... OK.

(STEVE gets to his shirt pocket and pulls out ...)

MEGAN. A condom? You have got to be kidding me.

(LULIE laughs.)

ELAINE. Oh please!

ROBBIE. Ready for a little safe sex up here, Steve?

STEVE. *(Blushing badly.)* No, I mean it was just there.

MEGAN. Just there? You just carry these in your shirt pocket?

STEVE. Yeh, as a matter of fact ...

LULIE. So what's Bud supposed to blow it up? *(Giggles.)*

BUD. Go to h... *(LARGE HICCUP.)*

MEGAN. *(After recovering from that one, SHE rips the packet open with her teeth and passes it up to Lulie. Urgently.)* Here Lulie, pull it out.

LULIE. *(Really giggling.)* Hope this is as bad for hiccups as it is for sex.

ELAINE. Is that the kind made out of sheep bladders?

STEVE. Uh ...

ROBBIE. Uh oh, you're not a vegetarian are you, Bud?

BUD. Robbie, you may not live to spend that two hundred dollars. *(HICCUP.)*

MEGAN. Here it is; here it is; here it is. Take it Bud.

STEVE. Bud, ya got nothing to lose, right?

BUD. *(Grabs rubber with a fury. Begins to huff and puff into it.)* Dang! Puff ... puff ... puff ...puuuuuuufff ... puff. *(HICCUP.)*

LULIE. Bud?

BUD. Puff ... puff, pufff. *(HICCUP.)*

LULIE. Bud, please try 'cause ... *(Growing slightly more hysterical.)* It's not just the publicity. I mean I do have to make a move if I'm ever going to catch the public eye.

BUD. Puff ... puff ... *(HICCUP.)*

MEGAN. Lulie do you think you're ...

LULIE. No let me say this. Bud! OK now listen this is important. I can't just fall down from here, Bud. I can't just throw this all away cause ... I'm pregnant!

(BUD and STEVE react simultaneously.)

    BUD. *(Lets the balloon fly way.)* What!!!?
    STEVE. What??!
(Beat of silence.)

    ROBBIE. This row is beginning to feel very crowded.
    MEGAN. Lulie, what in the world are you trying to pull?
    ELAINE. Steve, you're shaking, I don't think I can ...
    BUD. *(To Steve.)* What d'you mean what?
    STEVE. What d'you mean what do I mean what? What do *you* mean what?
    MEGAN. I'm beginning to have serious regrets.
    BUD and STEVE. Lulie!
    LULIE. Yes?

(BUD and STEVE speak simultaneously.)

    BUD. Are you saying that I ...
    STEVE. When did you start ...

(BUD and STEVE stare each other down.)

    LULIE. Notice anything?
    ROBBIE. Could you be a bit more specific, dear?
    LULIE. Notice any hiccups lately?

(Brief silence. ALL HEADS turn to BUD who looks out, concentrating.)

    ROBBIE. It's fairly quiet, Bud.
    ELAINE. *(Kindly.)* Lulie, when is your baby due?

(HEADS turn toward Lulie.)

LULIE. What baby?

STEVE and BUD. What d'you mean what baby?

LULIE. I was just trying Steve's story. You know that guy who got shot in the face?

MEGAN. Lulie!

LULIE. Well it scared him didn't it?

(General surprise and dismay.)

STEVE. I don't even want this two hundred dollars anymore.

BUD. You don't want the two hundred dollars? After what I've been through you don't want the two hundred dollars?

STEVE. I don't want to hear what you've been through. We've been busting our chops to help you, Buddy.

MEGAN. *(Getting bounced.)* I've got to hand it to you Lulie. At least with the hiccups it was only one of them.

LULIE. You guys! Cut it out. We've got some time to spend here together.

ROBBIE. We've got three hours and twenty-seven minutes to spend here together.

MEGAN. Lulie's right guys. Two hundred dollars is still two hundred dollars.

STEVE. I'm not saying a word.

BUD. That two hundred dollars better be in my hands by tomorrow. Fred! *(Calling down.)* Thanks again, pal.

(LIGHTS begin a very slow fade.)

LULIE. This'll be an achievement, something we'll never forget.

ELAINE. *(Dreaming.)* You know, I've heard that Minoan acrobats could hold a lift for up to twelve hours ... some of them even performed on the backs of bulls.

MEGAN. So what else is new?

ROBBIE. I wonder if the Minoans were as well equipped for medical emergencies.

LULIE. Do you see that van? Is that Channel 7? It is; it's the

Action Cam!

ROBBIE. Be sure to give them your best side, dear, whichever that may be.

(LULIE gives a squeal of anticipation.)

MEGAN. I'm beginning to think we might make this.

(LIGHTS are almost out.)

STEVE. A-CHOOO!
LULIE. Steve?
STEVE. AAAAACHOOO!

(BLACKOUT.)

MEGAN. Oooooh nooooo...

THE END

BED & BREAKFAST

by Richard Dresser

Bed & Breakfast premiered at the Actors Theatre of Louisville on June 5, 1989. It was directed by J. Christopher Wineman and had the following cast:

ALICE ....Marion Zweng
SARAH ....Mary Evans Lott
CHUCK...Jason O'Neill
CLAUDE ....M. Carl Kaufman
EVELYN..Moira Brennan

Scenic Designer: Paul Owen
Sound Designer: Mark Hendren
Property Master: Mark Bissonnette
Production Stage Manager: Carey Upton
Costume Designer: Kevin McLeod
Lighting Designer: Jan Thornsberry
Technical Director: Steve Goodin
Production Managers: Bob Krakower, J. Christopher Wineman
Dramaturg: Nancy Klementowski

CHARACTERS

SARAH   A young American woman
ALICE   An American woman of any age
EVELYN   A British woman of indeterminate age
CHUCK   Sally's husband, a thug
CLAUDE   Alice's husband

SETTING

The play is set on a spring morning in a modest bed and breakfast establishment in England. The time is the present.

We see the dining area, which includes perhaps three or four tables for the guests. A door leads to the kitchen, another door leads to the rooms.

BED & BREAKFAST

A bed and breakfast in England. Morning. Several tables with red and white checked tablecloths. At one of them sits SARAH, American, young, nervous, vulnerable, and terribly sad.
ALICE enters. SHE is very self-possessed, brisk, and efficient. SARAH smiles at her hopefully. ALICE barely acknowledges this with a cursory nod. SHE sits down at the other table and snaps open a newspaper with great authority. SARAH stares at her, trying to get up the nerve to speak. ALICE suddenly bellows toward the kitchen.

ALICE. I'm not going to sit here all day waiting! I want my coffee and I want it now! This is your last warning! (*Under her breath.*) Lazy good for nothing bastards.
SARAH. (*Full of wonder.*) Oh! You're an American!

(ALICE glances at her briefly.)

SARAH. I feel like I'm seeing an old friend even though we never met. Just the sound of a good old American voice, I must confess it warms my heart. I have such problems with the language here. Could you say something else? I don't care what it is, I just want to hear the sound of your voice.
ALICE. (*Yelling to the kitchen.*) Bring me the goddam coffee! I refuse to be treated this way!
SARAH. Thank you. My name is Sarah Greenwell. Well, actually, as of last week it's Sarah Greenwell Pitkin, due to the occasion of my marriage, my very first. What's your name, or maybe I should just sit quietly and mind my own business?
ALICE. Alice. (*To the kitchen.*) I'll give you 'til ten. Then I will not be responsible for my actions. One. Two. Three. Four.

(EVELYN enters. SHE is a very morose British woman.)

EVELYN. *(Heavy British accent.)* Me mum is sick, Miz Madison. I'm all alone in the kitchen trying to feed and clothe the twins for the day ahead—

ALICE. Oh, for God sakes, Evelyn, your mother's drunk and the twins are eighteen years old. I'd like my coffee now.

EVELYN. Right away, right away. *(An afterthought.)* If I had the courage I'd end it all. There's nothing left for me to live for, nothing at all. I'm nothing but a burden to myself and those around me. All I live for is my Final Reward.

ALICE. I'm still waiting on that coffee.

(EVELYN exits.)

SARAH. See what I mean about the way they talk? They all sound like they're on Public Television. *(Tentatively.)* What's it like over there now? In America, I mean. Where I'm from it's the first blush of spring. The time of year when I met Chuck Pitkin. I think about home all the time. The people are so friendly, and the television is better and they cook things right. Sometimes I think if I wished hard enough I could actually be there. Even if it's just for an instant. Isn't that silly?

ALICE. How long have you been over here, anyway?

SARAH. We got in Tuesday. It seems like forever.

ALICE. No wonder you're homesick.

SARAH. And lonely. Terribly terribly lonely.

ALICE. I was under the impression you just got married.

SARAH. Oh, yes, but, well, it hasn't been easy. You know, the silly little differences that don't seem so important until you get married. See, Chuck and I are from different backgrounds. My family owned the only factory in town. We were almost like royalty. People would practically bow down to us on the street. And Chuck, well, he came from a large family. They had nothing. They lived in a shack in the woods and sometimes they tried to sell things beside the road. Mainly useless junk or things they'd stolen. In the evening, all fifteen or sixteen of them would ride around in his daddy's pick-up, searching for road-kills. There was a barbecue in the back, and they'd grill them up, right there next to the road. He still thinks it's a luxury to eat an animal with no fur on it. Do you see what I'm up against?

ALICE. Well, I'm sure you can get used to each other.

(EVELYN enters with coffee. SHE's just about to put it down when ALICE stops her.)

ALICE. Wait! This coffee is terrible! Isn't it!

EVELYN. Yes, Miz Madison. I'm sorry.

ALICE. Take it back and make me a fresh cup, do you understand?

(EVELYN whimpers and exits.)

SARAH. How could you tell?

ALICE. It's always terrible. It saves time if I don't taste it.

SARAH. I don't like this place. Chuck is restless. He wants to move on. He says there's nothing here.

ALICE. There's Stonehenge.

SARAH. Oh, have you been?

ALICE. Every day.

SARAH. Really? Because we went and it was okay, but nothing moved or anything. It was just these rocks. I liked the gift shop. *(Gets out little rocks.)* See? I got my own little Stonehenges. Fourteen dollars, or maybe it was pounds. *(Beat.)* Why would you go every day?

ALICE. My husband likes it.

SARAH. Your husband! You must be married! Congratulations! *(Beat.)* Oh, God, what a stupid, stupid thing to say. Of course you're married if you have a husband.

(EVELYN enters with coffee for Alice, then starts to leave.)

SARAH. Oh, excuse me, miss, I'd like to order breakfast? This is breakfast-inclusive, isn't it?

EVELYN. What would you like?

SARAH. I'd like two poached eggs, with sausage on the side, a grapefruit, and two coffees. My husband likes his coffee first thing.

EVELYN. Toast?

SARAH. Whole wheat.

EVELYN. Very good. (*EVELYN exits with a smirk.*)

SARAH. Isn't that dear? She didn't even write it down.

ALICE. Why should she? We all get the same thing every morning, no matter what we order. I used to believe it made a difference, but it doesn't.

SARAH. Why do they—

ALICE. They think it's polite to pretend you can have whatever you want.

SARAH. How long have you been here?

ALICE. A long time. A very long time. Years.

SARAH. Why would you stay if this is the way they treat you?

ALICE. Stonehenge. My husband likes Stonehenge.

EVELYN. (*Enters with two bowls of porridge.*) Porridge?

ALICE and SARAH. Here!

EVELYN. (*Giving them the porridge.*) If I weren't around any longer the twins would have to take over the place. Make something of themselves. As long as I'm here they do nothing at all. I'm holding them back something terrible, and they're quick to tell me. I can hardly see through the black cloud that surrounds me. Oh, it's constant misery in my little corner of the world. (*EVELYN exits.*)

SARAH. I feel so much better the more I know of that woman's life. My little problems don't seem near so bad. (*Starts to sob.*)

ALICE. What is it?

SARAH. Nothing. Just ... I think Chuck is trying to kill me.

ALICE. No! Really?

SARAH. He refuses to drive on the left side of the road. He says he's been driving since he was ten and he'll be goddammed if a bunch of foreigners will tell him what to do. He just grits his teeth and barrels ahead and the other cars have to swerve out of the way. Everywhere we go we leave a trail of vehicles on their side next to the road. It's so embarrassing.

ALICE. You don't say anything?

SARAH. He won't listen. He says this is why we fought the war, so we can have personal freedom. What should I do? I think he wants to bump me off for my money. These odd things keep happening. I'm lucky to be alive. I don't know what to do. I promised to spend the rest of my life with him but I didn't think it would come so soon.

ALICE. (*Gets out pills.*) Put this in his coffee.

SARAH. What is it?

ALICE. My husband's medication.

SARAH. For what?

ALICE. To calm him down. He has this condition. He can only remember what's happened in the last fifteen minutes. Then it's all gone. Life begins all over for him every quarter hour.

SARAH. How awful!

ALICE. We prefer to think of it as a challenge. (*Looks at watch.*) If he isn't here soon then he'll forget how to find the dining room. He'll forget that we're married. That's why we always have to stay together ... so he'll remember.

SARAH. I wouldn't want to be you for anything in the whole world!

ALICE. Oh? Well *my* husband is not trying to kill me.

SARAH. I'm sorry. I'm not myself this morning. I'm not even anyone I know. (*SHE takes the pill from Alice as we hear CHUCK coming.*) What will this do to him?

ALICE. Loosen him up, break through his defenses and help him get to the truth.

(*SARAH tosses it in the coffee. CHUCK enters and sits down with Sarah. HE's a grim man who should be incarcerated.*)

SARAH. Good morning, honey!

CHUCK. Yeah? Is that what it is?

SARAH. Would you like some porridge?

CHUCK. Sure, that's what I'd like. Some goddam porridge. Maybe then we can eat some cement. (*Loudly.*) What I want is a freaking cheeseburger!

SARAH. I'll tell the girl.

CHUCK. We coulda gone anywhere and we come to this lousy little dump where all they speak is English. For Chrissakes we coulda gone to Florida, and you push this on me. Like it's going to make me a better person. No TV, no *USA Today*, let me tell you one thing, babe, you got your way now but I'll get my way in the end.

SARAH. Chuck! Please.

(SARAH gets up and goes to the kitchen. ALICE is reading her paper. CHUCK looks around, then furtively drops some pills in Sarah's coffee. SARAH comes back.)

SARAH. So ... what would you like to do today?

CHUCK. Maybe we can find some more funny rocks to stare at.

SARAH. Ssh! My friend Alice goes there every day!

CHUCK. (*Looks at her.*) That figures. (*Beat.*) I think I'll take the car, try to find a pub with a big screen TV. Maybe catch some bowling or something. Get drunk on my ass. Pick up some wench. Come back and wreck the room and puke on your clothes.

SARAH. What about me? This is my honeymoon, too.

CHUCK. I don't think you need to worry about planning your day.

SARAH. Why?

CHUCK. Let's just say I planned it for you.

ALICE. (*Looks at watch.*) Damn! I don't think he made it.

(Just then CLAUDE enters. HE looks a bit confused.)

ALICE. Hi, Claude. Over here.

(CLAUDE takes another table. HE nods at Alice without recognition.)

ALICE. It's me, honey. Alice.

(CLAUDE gets out a newspaper.)

CHUCK. *(To Alice.)* Give up, sister. He isn't interested.

(EVELYN enters with a bowl of porridge.)

CHUCK. I had the cheeseburger, medium rare.
EVELYN. Very good, sir. *(SHE puts the bowl of porridge in front of him.)* Me doctor says I'm in excellent health. "Miranda," he said, confusing me with my late sister, "you have the body of a young woman and the mind of a small child. I predict you live to one hundred and twenty." Don't be puttin' your curses on me, I replied. It's all I can do to drag myself through the afternoon. If I were nimble enough I'd leap in front of a speeding bus. *(EVELYN exits.)*
CHUCK. *(To Sarah.)* Does this look anything like a cheeseburger to you? Does it?
SARAH. I'm sorry, Chuck.
CHUCK. I need some male companionship. All this girl-talk is making me angry.

(HE goes over to Claude's table. SARAH is alone with her porridge, which SHE tries to eat.)

CHUCK. Hey, bud. On your own?
CLAUDE. I think so.
CHUCK. You wanna raise some hell today? Drink too much, drive too fast, buy some guns, see what happens?
CLAUDE. No thank you.
CHUCK. *(Shrugs.)* It's your life. *(CHUCK takes a big swig of coffee. The medication starts to hit him.)*
CLAUDE. *(To Chuck.)* Hey, do you know that woman over there?
CHUCK. Alice something. Frankly, I think you're wasting your time.
CLAUDE. I think she's a beauty. Would you mind introducing me?

CHUCK. Hey, Alice! Mind if this twerp talks to you?
ALICE. Not at all.

(With great ceremony, CLAUDE goes over to Alice's table. HE brings a flower that was in a vase on his table. SARAH watches this, envious.)

CLAUDE. My name is Claude.
ALICE. Hello, Claude. Won't you join me?
CLAUDE. I'd be delighted. (*HE sits down with her.*) I couldn't take my eyes off you from the time I walked in here. There's something about you. Something special.
ALICE. There's something about you, too, Claude.
CLAUDE. Are you traveling with someone?
ALICE. I'm all alone.
CLAUDE. You're the most beautiful woman I've ever seen. I hope you don't think I'm too forward, but I was wondering if you'd like to take a trip with me today. I got a brochure in the lobby. There's this place, not too far from here. An ancient place, full of mystery. Stonehenge. I'd like to see it ... and I'd like for you to go with me ... if you could.
ALICE. I'd love to. Thank you for asking. I think we should leave right away. I've heard it's better in the early morning, before all the tour busses show up.
CLAUDE. There's so much I want to know about you, Alice. I feel as though I've been looking for you my whole life.
ALICE. We've got all the time in the world, Claude.

(THEY smile at each other. Then THEY get up and leave, with ALICE taking his arm. SARAH is watching them.)

SARAH. Remember when it was like that, Chuck? Whatever happened to us?
CHUCK. *(Dreamily.)* I don't know. I don't know anything anymore. (*CHUCK sees SARAH about to drink her coffee.*) Sarah! Stop!
SARAH. What is it?

CHUCK. Don't drink that coffee!

SARAH. (*Puts the cup down.*) Chuck? Are you all right?

CHUCK. I feel so strange. So calm. Like I'm seeing things for the first time. There's poison in the coffee, Sarah. I put it there myself.

SARAH. You've been trying to kill me this whole honeymoon, haven't you?

CHUCK. Yes. But now I see it's something else I'm angry at. How hard my life has been, having to eat small animals, that kind of thing. It makes a man nasty. And you having everything. I start to hate you for loving me. And then I think "would I hate her less if she didn't love me as much?" And then I start to get confused. And when a man gets confused, he has to take immediate action. I'm sorry, Sarah. (*Beat.*) Why am I talking this way? I could be on any number of daytime talk shows.

SARAH. I put something in *your* coffee, Chuck.

CHUCK. What?

SARAH. It wasn't poison. Just some medication that Alice gave me when I told her you were trying to kill me.

CHUCK. Whatever it is, I want to hold onto this. I want to hold onto everything I know right now. I've spent my whole life trying to avoid what I now feel. (*Beat.*) Would you like to go to Stonehenge today?

SARAH. Stonehenge? You really want to go?

CHUCK. I think today I might understand it.

(*THEY stand up.*)

SARAH. Will you promise me one thing, Chuck?

CHUCK. Anything.

SARAH. Will you drive on the right side of the road?

CHUCK. Yes, darling. For you I will do that.

(*THEY leave, very much together, just as EVELYN enters from the kitchen. SHE sees the full cup of coffee on the table where Sarah was sitting. SHE picks it up.*)

EVELYN. Coffee's still no good?

(No response, as CHUCK and SARAH leave. EVELYN shrugs, drinks the coffee, piles up the dishes and goes into the kitchen. A beat, then an enormous CRASH. BLACKOUT.)

THE END

VISITING DAD

A short play for three actors

by Judith Fein

Visiting Dad played at the Actors Theatre of Louisville on June 17, 1991. It was directed by Bob Krakower and had the following cast:

MIKE ....Jay Rosenbloom
LAURA ....Olivia Honegger
DAD ....Jesse Wolfe

Scenic Design: Paul Owen
Lighting Designer: Matt Reinert
Costume Designer: Kevin McLeod
Sound Designer: Darron West
Property Master: Mark Bissonnette
Production Manager: Bob Krakower
Stage Manager: Emily Fox
Dramaturg: Emily F. Morse

VISITING DAD

MIKE and LAURA bowl downstage, facing the audience, on an imaginary lane. The SOUND TRACK provides ambience, bowling pins, etc. LAURA readies herself for her turn.

MIKE. Use the thumb. Use the leverage. Eyes down. Focus. Then let her rip.

LAURA. I can't believe I'm bowling.

MIKE. It's good for us. We can't be cerebral all the time. This is just you, the ball, the pins, the alley. Simple.

LAURA. (*Lets the ball rip. SHE lets out a disappointed groan.*) Gutter ball.

MIKE. C'mon. Try again.

LAURA. (*Laughing.*) Okay. (*SHE tries again. Again a groan and a sigh.*)

MIKE. It's only one turn. Forget it. (*HE picks up his ball.*)

LAURA. It's a bad omen. I think it's a metaphor. You rev up, you try, you land in the gutter.

MIKE. That's absurd. You probably just weren't concentrating.

LAURA. It IS a metaphor. You choose a ball at random, although there are many balls to choose from. You try to get a grip on it. You invest your hopes. It takes off on its own. You land in the gutter.

(MIKE laughs, holds his ball aside and kisses Laura lightly.)

MIKE. You're such a character. You never take things at face value. You always have to look *through* things to see what's really going on.

LAURA. Well, nothing's what it seems to be. There's this visible and apparent level of meaning—but it's usually a whitewash. If you peel it away—

MIKE. (*Puts down his ball and grabs Laura.*) I love it when

95

you talk like that! Give up your apartment and move in with me. Let's get married.

LAURA. What? This is our fifth date.

MIKE. I knew on our first date. You'll never bore me. You're amusing, you've got this great circuitous mind, you're sexy and best of all—you're limitless.

LAURA. It's much too soon.

MIKE. What are we waiting for?

LAURA. I can't move into your place. I've got a lot of furniture.

MIKE. Sell it. You said yourself the Santa Fe style is a dinosaur.

LAURA. How do we know our friends will get along?

MIKE. If they're your friends, they're extensions of you and I'll like them. If any of my friends don't like you—they're not my friends anymore.

LAURA. Go ahead. Bowl. It's your turn.

(Mike's ball tears down the lane.)

MIKE. Strike!

LAURA. Mike—I'll move in with you—

MIKE. Great! I knew it!

LAURA. —I'll move in with you if you meet my father and he agrees.

MIKE. Honey, I can humbly tell you that I am flawless with parents. They all want me to marry their daughters. When do you want me to meet him?

LAURA. Tonight. Right now.

MIKE. Not dressed like this.

LAURA. You don't have to dress for Dad.

MIKE. I'm sweaty. I'm smelly. I need a shower.

LAURA. My father's not concerned with appearances ... or smells.

MIKE. You sure?

LAURA. Very.

MIKE. Should we finish the game?

LAURA. (*Throws her ball and watches it roll down the alley.*) Gutter ball.

MIKE. Who cares? You're moving in with me.

LAURA. It's a sign, Mike. The universe puts out big neon signs and we're too blind to read them.

MIKE. WE'RE ONLY BOWLING!! IT'S ONLY A GUTTER BALL!!

(*BLACKOUT. Dim LIGHTS come up.*)

LAURA. Daddy, I'd like you to meet Mike. He's asked me to move in with him and get married.

(*LIGHTS come up further, revealing a tombstone in front of them. It reads. ED KAISER: 1924-1981. BELOVED FATHER.*)

MIKE. Oh, come on, Laura. This is like something out of a Halloween anthology.

LAURA. (*Dead serious; to her father.*) I went to see Mama last week and there were leaves all over the mound so I cleared them off and I left a chalk mark on the stone to show I was there, just like you used to do.

MIKE. Laura, this is spooky. Why didn't you tell me your parents were dead? I'm really sorry. It must be very hard on you having lost both of them. I mean, my parents are so important to me.

LAURA. Daddy, no matter what happened between you and Mama, she never should have asked to be buried with her family. It's not right. She belongs here. Even if things aren't settled. There's something so—final—and macabre about that cemetery. It even smells like death.

MIKE. Are you sure it's a good idea for you to come here? Doesn't it dig up the pain for you?

LAURA. (*To Mike.*) First I address him alone, and then you get a chance to speak. There's an order to things we have to respect.

MIKE. You've done this before?

LAURA. Every man who's been interested in me has had to

meet my father.

MIKE. How many was that?

LAURA. Eight. Nine. Maybe ten. I don't remember.

MIKE. And what happened?

LAURA. I'm still single, thank God. I could have made a ghastly mistake. My parents had a very unhappy marriage. It keeps us all vigilant so we don't repeat the pattern. (*Pointedly.*) I told you. Things may seem fine on the surface. Everyone thought my parents were ideally suited, but they're rarely what they seem. (*To her father.*) I hope you're comfortable, Daddy. I had them change from annual to perennial care. Now I know you'll be weeded and kept clean forever. My only regret is that I didn't have a photo of you set into the granite stone so future generations could see how handsome you were. Your deep, ivy-green eyes, your mustache—

MIKE. Laura, honey, I'm sorry you had to go through so much loss and pain.

LAURA. (*To Mike.*) Shhhh. Never interrupt. It introduces static into the channel. (*To her father.*) Daddy, do you agree to meet Mike?

(*The WIND blows.*)

LAURA. He's agreed. Why don't you start by introducing yourself?

MIKE. I don't have much practice at this.

LAURA. Just speak from the heart.

MIKE. (*To father.*) Sir, my name is Mike Trabulo. I work in advertising. I'm with a big firm but I expect to go out on my own within the next few years. I like classical music, fly fishing, sailing on a breezy day—

LAURA. (*Whispering.*) He's getting restless. Talk to him about what matters.

MIKE. Jesus. (*Beat.*) Okay, I'll try. This really isn't easy. (*To father.*) Sir, I love your daughter very much and I want to marry her. I'll take good care of her and you'll never have to worry about her happiness or safety.

LAURA. (*Low.*) Good, Mike.

FATHER'S VOICE. Michael Trabulo, have you ever been married before?

(MIKE looks around. No one is there except for Laura. HE blanches.)

LAURA. Don't be afraid. The dead just seem to be silent but if you observe certain rules and open the channels, they always answer back.

MIKE. *(Whispering to Laura.)* Okay. *(To father.)* No, sir.

F's VOICE. You're lying, Trabulo.

MIKE. It wasn't really a marriage, sir.

LAURA. What? When were you married?

MIKE. It was nothing ... it was a disaster ... I had forgotten about it, sir.

LAURA. How long were you married?

MIKE. No time. Months. Weeks. It seemed like hours.

F'S VOICE. WHY did she want a divorce after two and a half years, Trabulo?

MIKE. I really don't want to go into that, if you don't mind. It was the past, sir. I have every intention of discussing it with Laura when the time is—

F'S VOICE. NOW!!

MIKE. *(Low.)* She was disgusted. *(Beat.)* So was I. So am I. I swear it.

F'S VOICE. You didn't ACT on your desires? In the street? Behind a telephone pole? In the school yard when little kids were getting out of school?

MIKE. No. On my honor. It wasn't like that. I never did it outside the house. It was harmless.

LAURA. Did what?

MIKE. Laura, let's get out of here.

F'S VOICE. Nylons and garter belts. That's how it started.

MIKE. *(Thunderstruck.)* How do you know that?

F'S VOICE. When we die, we dematerialize. What do you think guilt and shame REALLY are? They are the unconscious knowledge and recognition that the dead see and know all that you do. Everything. There's nothing you can hide.

MIKE. (*To father.*) After the stockings and garter belt, I bought a woman's hat at an auction. It was made of black silk and cream-colored lace. I paid a fortune for it. I waited to get home every night so I could put it on.

F'S VOICE. And the dress? The wig?

MIKE. I had them made. They were beautiful. It didn't hurt anyone. Please understand me ... it wasn't a sexual thing. Women are so vulnerable. Everyone wants to take care of them. I wanted to experience that. (*To Laura.*) I never do it anymore. It's over. I disgust myself.

(*LAURA grimaces at the revelation.*)

F'S VOICE. DO YOU STILL DO IT ALL THE TIME?

MIKE. I promise, it's over. I mean ... it's sporadic. And it only happens in the most private reaches of my innermost mind. Sometimes, just to get started, I picture—I imagine—that they're the man and I'm the woman.

F'S VOICE. DO YOU DO IT WITH MY DAUGHTER LAURA?

MIKE. Laura's different. I want to marry her. To spend my life with her.

LAURA. Do you, Mike?

MIKE. (*Turns slowly to Laura. HE almost stutters.*) I'm ... Laura, I ... sometimes I feel this pressure crushing on my chest. It's more than I can bear. If you initiate or if I close my eyes and pretend that you initiate, it takes the pressure off.

LAURA. I hate to initiate. I do it all day at work. When I come home from a hard day at the office, I need to be passive.

MIKE. Fine. You don't have to DO anything. I work it out in my head. It's between me and me. It's harmless.

F'S VOICE. Five visits to a fertility specialist.

MIKE. She wanted to have children. That was years ago.

F'S VOICE. Low sperm motility.

MIKE. (*To Laura.*) IT WAS STRESS. (*Distraught; to father.*) Sir, it was an erroneous medical diagnosis. You know how often doctors are wrong. They only look at the results, but they ignore the cause. There's nothing wrong with my sperm. They could swim upstream like salmon. If the demands were gone. With the right woman. (*Tender.*)With Laura.

LAURA. We've never talked about children.

MIKE. Do you want them?

LAURA. On the one hand, children give you immortality. But on the other hand, they crush you further and further into a corner where you can't breathe and the life is sucked out of you.

F'S VOICE. The hole in your resume, Mike. The blank space between 1986 and 1987.

MIKE. I lay in bed, sir. I read Kierkegaard and Joseph Campbell, Lao-Tsu, Melville, Archie and Veronica comics. I decorated t-shirts. I drew arcane designs and sent them to friends. I felt myself dissolve into Jello—mint-green, aqueous, vaguely transparent. I oozed over the bed and onto the floor. And just as I was turning to liquid a voice said to me, "Not yet, Mike." And I turned my life around, sir. You're looking at a changed man.

LAURA. You've had such pain, Mike. Great, great pain.

MIKE. But, sir, Laura, if I hadn't gone through it, I would never know what joy was. If I hadn't been Jello, I could never have loved Laura. I would have gone on the way I was.

F'S VOICE. The cord and the grave, Mike.

MIKE. Oh, God. You saw that too?

F'S VOICE. We don't sleep. Even when you sleep, we are hyper-vigilant. Every earthly action is observed on another plane.

MIKE. I was strangled by my past. I read every self-help book. I was in therapy. I kept a journal. I went to seminars. But nothing could break the hold. One morning I went to a park. It was 4 a.m. I brought with me a huge length of mariner's rope. I tied one side to a tree and the other side around my waist. I ran back and forth until I was aching and raw from the rope cutting into me and then when I couldn't stand it anymore, I pulled out a pocket knife and cut the cord that bound me to my mother.

LAURA. Symbolically?

MIKE. No. Literally. Then I got down on my hands and knees and I dug and dug in the dirt until my hands were bleeding. I sang

a prayer for the dead I learned in church as a child. Then I said a
sad and bitter farewell and buried my father.

LAURA. Your father's still alive. So it was symbolic.

MIKE. No. I really buried him. I watched him die.

LAURA. (*To her father.*) You see my dilemma, Dad. He wants
me to move in and marry him.

F'S VOICE. My verdict is: He's a gutter ball.

LAURA. I'm sorry, Mike.

F'S VOICE. Marry him.

LAURA and MIKE. WHAT?

F'S VOICE. The path you will walk together will be full of
stones and brambles, but it will be interesting. He is a man who
doesn't run from the living or the dead. He is precisely what you
need, Laura. He is much, much more than he seems.

LAURA. Daddy? (*There is no answer.*) Daddy? (*To Mike.*) The
channel's not open anymore. (*Beat.*) You're the first man I've ever
brought here that he's approved of.

MIKE. That was very difficult.

LAURA. Selling my furniture won't be a piece of cake.

MIKE. I guess we'll just go ahead and deal with it.

LAURA. (*Faces him, grabs his face in her hands, and kisses
him.*) You're a YES person, Mike. You say YES, YES, YES to
whatever life throws in your path. All I've ever known is NO men.
That's why my father approves of you. And that's why I love you.
I'm ready to move in!

MIKE. You think the dead will be watching us?

LAURA. Of course they will. They always are.

MIKE. (*To all the dead.*) Well, welcome, guys. (*Beat; reflects.*)
Yes, yes, yes, A wonderful wife and a direct line to the dead. I
think I could get into this ...

(*THEY kiss lovingly. Then, after a beat—*)

MIKE. Laura ... I don't have to meet your mother, do I?

LAURA. It's not fair that you just meet one and not the other.
(*SHE takes MIKE by the hand and starts to lead him offstage.*)
She's very different from Daddy. She's passive and moody and not

very talkative. She rarely expresses herself, but she seethes inside ...

(MIKE follows her. THEY exit to visit mother as we BLACKOUT.)

THE END

AMERICAN WELCOME

by Brian Friel

American Welcome premiered at the Actors Theatre of Louisville on February 27, 1980. It was directed by Michael Hankins and had the following cast:

The American ....Anthony Heald
The European..William McNulty

Set Design: Paul Owen
Costume Design: Kurt Wilhelm
Lighting Design: Jeff Hill
Co-Property Masters Sam Garst, Sandra Strawn
Stage Manager: Benita Hofstetter

AMERICAN WELCOME

An hotel lobby. Piped MUSIC in background.
Two chairs, one on each side of a small table. On one chair sits the
EUROPEAN, a large brown envelope on his lap. HE casually
surveys his surroundings.
After a few seconds the AMERICAN enters, carrying a briefcase.
HE looks around, spots the European, bears down on him. The
American is young. HE speaks very rapidly and gives excessive
emphasis to several words in each sentence.

AMERICAN. It *is* Mr. Smith, isn't it? Mr. John Smith? I'd
recognize that distinguished head anywhere! I'm Bert—remember?
We've corresponded. I'm directing your play. Welcome, sir!
Welcome to America!

(THEY shake hands.)

AMERICAN. No-no. Don't get up—please. (*HE sits.*) May I?
Well! You've made it! You're here! Gosh! And may I tell you,
sir, how honored and how privileged we are to have you here with
us.
I'm sure you're still groggy with jet lag, are you? Can I get you
something to eat, something to drink? How's your hotel? Had you
a good flight? Can I get you a coffee? Tea? Beer? May I call you
Joe? Thank you. And may I make a personal comment? You look
so European—it's uncanny! (*Without breaking his speech HE*
opens his briefcase and takes out a script and a large note-block.)
Wonderful. Okay. Let's get down to business. But before we do,
Jim, may I tell you just once more how magnificent, how truly
magnificent your play is—I mean that—and how honored and
privileged I am to be associated with it. I really mean that. You
see, Bill, what you have given us is a perfectly conceived and
perfectly executed analysis of the human condition the world over.

It's so perfect it—it—it's frightening. Beautiful form. Electrifying language. Subtle wit. Penetrating insights. I mean to say that's art—that's real art—that's European art, if you know what I mean. What I'm trying to say, Tom, is this: you have entrusted me with this delicate perfection—and I'm scared. I say to myself: Bert, can you handle it? Are you worthy of it?

You're tired. Can I get you something? Coffee? Tea? Beer?

Okay. Fine. What have I got here? A few questions. Do you mind if I ask you a few silly questions? Just for my own enlightenment. I knew you wouldn't mind. And may I tell you, Chuck, how honored and how privileged we are to have you here with us? First problem: language. Frankly we're uneasy with the language. I mean to say we're not uneasy with the language—it's just that there's a lot of it we don't understand. Simply a question of usage: or to be more accurate, simply a question of our ignorance of your usage. I've made a list here—words like "boot," "bumper," "chemist"—there are maybe a dozen of them. Frankly we don't know what you mean. And since you want to communicate with American audiences and since we want them to understand you, I mean to say what we did was this. We went to our most distinguished American playwright—and you've got to meet him while you're here; he just adores your work—and what he did for us was this. He took all those little confusing words— five or six thousand approximately—and with wonderful delicacy and skill and with the utmost respect for the rhythms and tones of your speech, he did this most beautiful job of translating the play into the language we speak and understand. I hope you'll approve. I know you'll approve.

Can I get you something? Coffee? Tea? Beer? Gosh! I really can't believe it, Mike! You're actually here! I'm just knocked-out!

Okay. Second problem: the form of your play. We're uneasy with the form. I mean to say we're not uneasy with the form—it's just that you've written this wonderful naturalistic play but you've written it in monologue form! A naturalistic play in monologue form, for God's sake! I mean to say a monologue is just not naturalistic if you don't mind my saying so. Let me qualify that instantly. The monologue may be naturalistic in Europe but it is not "natural" to us. We talk, we exchange, we communicate. And since you want to communicate with American audiences and since we want them to understand you, I mean to say what we did was this. We went to our most distinguished American playwright—and you've got to meet him while you're here; he just reveres your work—and what he did for us was this. He took your little monologue and with wonderful delicacy and skill and with the utmost respect for the rhythms and tones of your speech, he did this most beautiful job of transforming your script into a four-character, two-act, single-set comedy that is just—how can I tell you?—just breathtaking. I hope you'll approve. I know you'll approve.

You're suffering from jet-lag—I can see it. Can I get you something? Gin? Whisky? Brandy? Gosh! I really can't believe it, Dan! You're actually here! I'm just knocked-out! (*HE sits back, relaxes, smiles contentedly.*) Well, that wasn't too bad now, was it? And here we are, all set to go. And let me tell you this. We think— hell, we know!—that we've got the most distinguished, the funniest, the most sensitive, the most disturbing, the most enlightening and the most moving play of the season—a big, big, big hit that is going to make us all rich and famous.

And may I tell you once more how honored and how privileged we are to have you here with us. May I shake that distinguished hand again?

Welcome, Tony Brown, welcome to America! (*HE takes the European's hand and pumps it with enthusiasm.*)

THE END

WHAT SHE FOUND THERE

by
John Glore

What She Found There is the co-winner of the Actors Theatre of Louisville 1990 Heideman Award and National Ten-Minute Play Contest.

What She Found There premiered at the Actors Theatre of Louisville on March 5, 1991. It was directed by Jon Jory and had the following cast:

LOU ....V Craig Heidenreich
CELIA ....Jennifer Hubbard

Costume Designer: Hollis Jenkins-Evans
Stage Manager: Lori M. Doyle
Dramaturg: Chiori Miyagawa
Scenic Designer: Paul Owen
Lighting Designer: Karl Haas
Sound Designer: Darron West
Props Master: Ron Riall

TIME & PLACE

The action takes place in a motel room. The time is the present.

WHAT SHE FOUND THERE

A low-rent motel room. The floor is covered by downtrodden carpet squares in a checker-board pattern. A man's shirt has been draped over the mirror on the dresser. On the upstage wall above the bed hangs a painting depicting all the king's horses and all the king's men trying to put Humpty-Dumpty back together again.

As the LIGHTS come up, CELIA, a young lady who looks and is dressed exactly like the famous Tenniel etchings of Lewis Carroll's Alice, is just pulling up her left stocking and straightening the horizontal stripes. SHE hums happily to herself. LOU, a nondescript, slightly ragged man in his twenties is still in bed, apparently naked under the covers. HE looks at Celia with a vaguely troubled expression.*

LOU. (*Pause.*) This was *how* long ago?
CELIA. (*Faintly British.*) One hundred and twenty years.

(Pause.)

LOU. Now wait. Lem-me see if I got this straight. She climbed up on the fireplace thing—
CELIA. —the mantle—
LOU. —and she went *through* the mirror—
CELIA. (*Correcting him.*) —looking-glass—
LOU. —right through it without breaking the glass and ended up on the other side. And *you* ... (*HE makes a vague gesture with his arms.*)
CELIA. ... came out. *I* came out. I passed through *her*, to be precise, my head through her head, my breast through her breast, my hips through her hips, and my toes through her toes. Not at all an unpleasant sensation, after the initial shock—rather like being squeezed out of a tube of tooth cream.

113

NOTE: In the tradition of other Alice plays, Celia is actually portrayed by a young adult.

LOU. And you've been wandering around in the real world ever since.

CELIA. No, I've been wandering around in *this* world ever since.

LOU. One hundred and twenty years.

CELIA. Yes.

(Pause.)

LOU. How come you look so young?

CELIA. As long as I'm in your world I don't age. She doesn't either, for that matter, while she's in Looking-Glass World.

LOU. Jesus, you telling me I just made it with a hundred-thirty-year-old woman?

CELIA. If you'd care to look at it that way. Of course I have the body of a thirteen-year-old.

LOU. Tell me about it. *(Pause.)* You know, before—the way you talked and all, you seemed like—I thought you were older, *much* older. Than thirteen, I mean. I thought you were, like, young for your age.

CELIA. And so I am. *(SHE smiles. Pause.)* I so enjoyed playing with your puppy, Louis.

LOU. You what again?

CELIA. Your puppy. It's a naughty little thing, but then they all are. I m sorry if I hurt its feelings when I giggled, but it has such a funny little pouty little mouth.

LOU. There you go with that "little" stuff again.

CELIA. My apologies. *(Beat.)* Of course *your* puppy doesn't talk.

(Beat.)

LOU. No.

CELIA. Back in Looking-Glass World my uncle's puppy used to talk to me all the time, and it said the most impertinent things! Needless to say, he wasn't really my uncle.

LOU. Right.

CELIA. But *your* puppy doesn't make any noise at all.

LOU. Well—

CELIA. (*Gleefully.*) And now I shall recite a poem for you! (*Launching into it forthwith.*) In the garden, late at night—

LOU. —Whoa, whoa!—

CELIA.
I found my way by candlelight
To a secret place which no one knows
Where the giggle sleeps and the yumyum glows.
Past the pussy-willows and—

LOU. Stop already!

CELIA. What is it?

LOU. You know on this side of the mirror we usually light up a cigarette or something.

CELIA. Beg pardon?

LOU. *After.* You know. We don't go in much for poems.

CELIA. I see. You don't wish to hear the rest, then?

LOU. Maybe later.

(*CELIA pouts, turning her back to him and making designs on the floor with the toe of her shoe.*)

LOU. Look, it's nothing personal, it's just—I'm kinda discombobulated is all. I mean I've heard some weird stories before, but—

(*SHE continues to pout, back turned.*)

LOU. So. You do this kinda thing often?

CELIA. (*Still pouting.*) Not at all. I've never done it before.

LOU. Oh *Christ*, now you're telling me I just made it with a hundred-thirty-year-old virgin!

CELIA. (*Turning and giggling.*) Don't be silly! I've done *that*. I've just never done it in a bed.

LOU. Where'd—

CELIA. Oh, behind the Times Square Coca-Cola sign, in the control tower of John Wayne International Airport, in the batter's

box at—
LOU. Okay, okay.

(*Pause.*)

CELIA. (*Not able to resist adding.*) Twice at Disneyland. (*Singing.*) It's a small world after all.
LOU. How many guys would you say you've—
CELIA. Hundreds. And you, Louis, do you always use the bed?
LOU. (*Defensive.*) Yeah!—well—once on a fuzzy rug in the—
CELIA. (*Delighted.*) How peculiar you are, Louis!

(*HE has grabbed his undershorts and is putting them on under the covers.*)

CELIA. Careful your little puppy doesn't bite you.
LOU. Right. Listen, I really enjoyed this and everything—
CELIA. Are you going to woo me now?
LOU. Woo you.
CELIA. It's customary. In Looking-Glass World, after the boy has his way with a girl he has never met before, he proceeds to woo her, beginning with passionate kisses and working his way gradually to exchange of pleasantries and courteous introductions. And then they part forever. The old ways are still the best, Louis, don't you agree?
LOU. Look, I was just—I don't know if I'm ready for, like you say, pleasantries and courteous whatevers.
CELIA. Everything in its time. (*SHE has wandered over to the window where SHE lifts a slat of the venetian blinds and peers out.*) I'm so glad you picked me up when you did. I was exhausted by the bewildering talk of that dirty woman with the shopping cart. She did seem quite certain, however, in her prognostications about the end of the world.
LOU. Crazy old bat.
CELIA. What is it that you're transporting in your lorry?
LOU. In my what?
CELIA. Your lorry, your "truck."

LOU. Oh. Hazardous waste. Hauling it to the dumpsite upstate.

CELIA. Hazardous waste. I once thought that referred to banana peels on sidewalks—tin cans with jagged lids, things of that sort. (*Still looking outside.*) Oh look! That boy is brandishing a windshield wiper and expostulating with great fervor to a fire hydrant. At last a breath of sanity in this senseless world!

LOU. (*Pulling on his trousers.*) Prob'ly on angel dust.

CELIA. Angel dust? Yes, we have that in Looking-Glass World, too. I once sprinkled some on a hitching post and it turned forthwith into a heliotrope.

LOU. Yeah, well, this ain't that kind of angel dust.

CELIA. (*Turning from the window.*) How this wiper-wielding warrior makes me long for my Looking-Glass home!

(*SHE has become sad. HE studies her for a moment.*)

LOU. Why don't you go back?

CELIA. I can't, of course. I must wait for *her*, and she will never come back now. She knows full well that we both would crumble into dust as soon as we returned to our rightful sides of the looking-glass. So I must continue to live in this backward world and do my best to forget what I've left behind.

LOU. That why you covered up the mirror?

(*SHE doesn't answer. Suddenly her mood changes again, but there's a willful edge to her cheer.*)

CELIA. Shall we play a game of wormy-wiggle? What fun! (*SHE delivers the following in a manic burst while SHE turns chairs upside down, scatters towels and clothing over the floor, knocks over a lamp, etc. By the end of the speech, the room is a shambles.*) Now the rules are really very simple, Louis, so pay attention, the object of the game being to outfox one's opponent through a carefully developed subterfuge involving randomly chosen items from the environment arranged in such a way as to disguise the true nature of the player's emotional landscape, your objective on the other hand being to unearth the subterranean secret by means of intuition, canny examination of archaeological artifacts, and a series of yes or no questions, with a time limit to be agreed upon by both contestants prior to start of game, after which we change sides and the rules are completely disintegrated in favor of general anarchy and wild good fun. Ready? (*SHE takes in his expression of utter exasperation.*) Oh you've guessed the secret already, haven't you?! What's the point of playing when I'm not allowed to win.

(Pause.)

  LOU. I'd better hit the road.

(Gets up, looks for his t-shirt under the bed, finds it, puts it on. CELIA looks around at the cluttered room.)

  CELIA. Do you know what I like least about this place, Louis?
  LOU. Hey look, it was convenient and cheap.
  CELIA. (*Not hearing him.*) Entropy. The tendency of all things in your world to move away from order towards chaos. In my own world, it's the opposite. Dust floats up off one's furniture and through the air and gradually drifts together to be molded by the wind into great mountain ranges. Swarms of locusts descend upon a barren field and then lift away again, leaving waves of wheat behind them. Ancient monuments rise up out of ruins and, as time passes, become pristine and proud. A hole in the knee of a little girl's stocking grows smaller and smaller until it disappears altogether. And of course as the people of Looking-Glass World grow older, they *find* their innocence. What a muddle.

(SHE plops onto the edge of the bed. Her sadness has become deep and very old. LOUIS looks at her. HE ambles over to the dresser. HE removes his shirt, revealing the mirror. HE looks at himself as HE puts on the shirt and buttons it. HE turns and looks around at the mess in the room. HE tells the following as though it's an amusing anecdote; SHE begins to listen as though it's a fairy tale.)

LOU. One time, when I was a kid, it was just me and my dad and his dad living in a one-bedroom place, and Dad and Grampa always used to go out drinking. They were both drunks. Anyway, this one night I was home alone, I was about thirteen, fourteen, and I decided to drink a six-pack of beer. You know: "I'll show them." So I did, I drank all six cans. By about the fourth can I was feeling pretty crazy, and I started trashing the place, turned over all the furniture, spilled food, papered everything with TP—basically turned the place upside-down. After the fifth can I was crying cause ... I guess I just felt really bad about messing things up. And after the sixth can I got sick. Barfed on the linoleum floor in the kitchen, went into the bedroom and passed out. Later on, I heard my dad and Grampa come in. They yelled at each other for awhile, then the door slammed and my dad's yelling disappeared down the street. The place got real quiet but then all of a sudden I heard this heavy thump. It scared me. I got out of bed and snuck back out into the living room but nobody was there. So I turned and looked in the kitchen and I saw my grampa. He had slipped on my puke, and he was just lying there on the floor, kinda bumbling around. He looked like one of those turtles on its back—trying to turn the world rightside up again. (*Laughs humorlessly.*) I just looked at him. He was really messed up, mumbling, groping—he coulda been hurt bad for all I knew. But I just looked at him. *I* was the *kid* ... My grampa, he used to play the piano, you know, jazz, classical, when he was a young man. I guess he was really good, cause he was gonna maybe go on tour or something. But then he had to take a factory job during the Depression, to support Gramma and my dad. He lost parts of three fingers in the machines. Couldn't play anymore after that. So. That's my story.

(*Pause.*)

CELIA. (*Still in story-land.*) Was your granddad a land turtle, a sea turtle or a mock turtle?
LOU. (*Smiling for the first time.*) Mock turtle, I guess.
CELIA. Yes, I thought so. (*Matter-of-fact.*) I'm sorry I never

knew your granddad, but I do know that in Looking-Glass World he never stopped playing the piano.

LOU. (*Turning to look in the mirror.*) Yeah?...

CELIA. Furthermore, most of the really great Looking-Glass musicians have some turtle in them.

LOU. (*Sitting down next to her.*) You know, I don't think you're half as strange as you make out to be.

CELIA. Yes, well, after a hundred-twenty years, I suppose a certain degree of assimilation would be inevitable. (*Pause.*) Would you like to go again? We can do it in the bed, if you want.

LOU. I think maybe I'd rather hear your poem now.

CELIA. (*With a giggle.*) Why Louis, you impetuous mandrill! You must put me in the proper mood first!

LOU. Then tell me your name.

CELIA. (*Suddenly shy.*) I'm called Celia.

LOU. Celia. (*Pause.*) It is a great pleasure to make your acquaintance, Celia.

CELIA. (*SHE blushes.*) Thank you, Louis.

(*THEY sit next to each other quietly, looking at their thoughts in the mirror. The LIGHTS fade to black.*)

THE END

EYE TO EYE

by
Christopher Graybill

Eye To Eye premiered at the Actors Theatre of Louisville on June 11, 1990. It was directed by William McNulty and had the following cast:

MAN ....Jeremy Gold
WOMAN ....Marta Johnson
WAITER ....Bruce Marshall Romans

Scenic Designer: Paul Owen
Lighting Designer: Jan Thornsberry
Costume Designers: Kevin McLeod
Sound Designer: Mark Hendren
Property Master: Mark Bissonnette
Production Manager: Bob Krakower
Stage Manager: Hannah Vesenka
Dramaturgs: Mary Samson

CHARACTERS

MAN
WOMAN
WAITER

TIME & PLACE

A restaurant. Present.

EYE TO EYE

As the play opens, the MAN and WOMAN have finished dinner at a
fashionable restaurant. HE reaches across the table toward her
hand, though HE does not touch her, and gazes into her eyes.

WOMAN. That's enough.
MAN. What's enough?
WOMAN. Stop, please.
MAN. Stop what?
WOMAN. Looking at me.
MAN. I like looking at you.
WOMAN. I can see that.
MAN. Don't you like it?
WOMAN. Sort of.
MAN. You like it. You love it.
WOMAN. Up to a point.
MAN. Set by you?
WOMAN. Who else?

(Beat.)

MAN. So you don't like my looks. I like yours. There are flecks
of brown in your right eye. Did you know that?
WOMAN. Yes.
MAN. They are very beautiful, your eyes.
WOMAN. Only the part you can see. My eyeballs are red-
veined, elongated bulbs of jelly. Just like yours.
MAN. Please, I just ate. How come it bothers you? My looking
at you. No, really. I'm interested.
WOMAN. It's too intimate.
MAN. Intimate? We're just sitting here. Having coffee. I'm
way over here.
WOMAN. There's something in your eye.

MAN. What?
WOMAN. I can't quite recognize it.
MAN. Something in my eye. Let me see now. Is it a gnat?
WOMAN. No.
MAN. An eyelash?
WOMAN. It's something hidden.
MAN. Something warm? Something cool? Something sexy?
WOMAN. Not exactly.
MAN. Bedroom eyes?
WOMAN. More than that.
MAN. That's interesting. That's very, very interesting.

(WAITER enters.)

WAITER. How was everything this evening?
WOMAN. Fine, thank you.
MAN. Fascinating.
WAITER. Can I bring you anything else?
MAN. I'd like more coffee.
WOMAN. Just the check, please.

(WAITER nods and exits.)

MAN. You double-parked?
WOMAN. Hmmm.

(THEY sit briefly in silence until the WAITER returns.)

WAITER. Here we are. (*HE refills Man's cup and leaves check.*) I'll take that whenever you're ready. (*HE exits.*)
WOMAN. *(Picking up check.)* I'll get this.
MAN. No, my treat. (*HE snatches the check from her hand.*)
WOMAN. Why don't we split it?
MAN. No, no, no, no. I treat you, then you treat me. That's the way it works around here.
WOMAN. I really would rather…
MAN. You're welcome. (*HE takes a credit card out of his*

wallet and places it on top of the bill.) You can get it next time.

WOMAN. Wait a minute. You better let me split it now. There isn't going to be a next time.

(THEY look at each other a moment.)

MAN. I see. OK. Tell you what. I've got a deal for you.

WOMAN. No, thanks.

MAN. A sporting proposition.

WOMAN. How much is my half?

(During the following exchange, SHE repeatedly reaches for the check, and HE holds it away.)

MAN. No, no. Let's do this fair and square. We both want to pay. We'll compete for it. Loser pays.

WOMAN. This is a boy's game.

MAN. We'll have a looking contest. Whoever breaks eye contact first, loses. *(Pause.)* Well?

WOMAN. Loser pays the check?

MAN. Bingo.

WOMAN. You're on. Ready?

MAN. Wait a minute. Let me get loose here. *(Does facial and neck exercises.)* The World Eyeballing Championships. All right. The Kid is ready. Here we go. On your mark, get set, stare!

WOMAN. *(Immediately averting her eyes.)* OK, I lose. Give me the check.

MAN. Oh, no. Time out.

WOMAN. I lost, fair and square. Hand it over.

MAN. No. I see what's happening here. I get it. We're going to have to revise the rules. *Winner* picks up the check.

WOMAN. I really want to leave.

MAN. Then leave! Walk out! Allow me the great honor of paying for you. Let me treat you. It would be my pleasure. *(Pause.)* Are you going to play or not?

WOMAN. I'll play.

(SHE takes out her credit card. THEY lay their gold American Express cards on the table.)

MAN. Ah, victory. Gold vs. gold. At last we see eye to eye.
WOMAN. Just start.
MAN. Go!

(THEY begin.)

MAN. Ho, ho, what a glare. Daggers, bullets. You won't be able to keep that up for long. You know what you look like?
WOMAN. Do you have to talk?
MAN. Why not? Nobody said anything about talking. There's nothing in the rules about talking. As I was saying, you look like one of those gargoyles whose stare turns men to stone.
WOMAN. Gorgon.
MAN. What?
WOMAN. It's a Gorgon, not a gargoyle.
MAN. Well, you must be a Gorgon because you are definitely turning me to stone.
WOMAN. You feel something getting hard?
MAN. Absolutely.
WOMAN. Maybe it's your arteries.
MAN. Ho, ho. Very good. But you don't get any style points.

(WAITER enters, notices their intensity and hesitates.)

WAITER. Can I take that for you? *(No response.)* No problem. Just let me know when you're ready. *(HE exits.)*
MAN. Your eyes are quivering. You're blinking fast. It won't be long now. Any second now you'll lose it. Ha, you looked away.
WOMAN. I did not.
MAN. Almost. You will.
WOMAN. Everything is a covert operation with men, isn't it?
MAN. Don't lecture me about "men."
WOMAN. All right, you. Let's talk about you. Nothing can be straightforward with you. It's all innuendo.

MAN. I never said that.

WOMAN. Your secret weapon is secrecy. You think what's unspoken is the biggest threat there is. But you're wrong.

MAN. Cheap shots. Nothing but cheap shots.

WOMAN. You never say what's on your mind.

MAN. How would you know?

WOMAN. I can see it in your eyes. Oh, it's not sex. I see that now. Sex is for teenagers. You're way past that.

MAN. What is it then?

WOMAN. I don't think you want me to say it.

MAN. Go ahead.

WOMAN. Not out loud.

MAN. As loud as you want.

WOMAN. Control. Domination. That's what's been in your eyes.

MAN. Is that the best you can do?

WOMAN. Sex is your means, not your end. (*Louder.*) You're thinking. I want to fuck this woman.

MAN. No fair.

WOMAN. (*Louder.*) I want to fuck her *into submission.*

WAITER. (*Enters anxiously.*) Are we OK here? Can I take that for you? Sir?

(*MAN looks up at Waiter.*)

WOMAN. You lose.

(*MAN hesitates, holding the check. Then HE reaches to take her credit card, and SHE hands it to him.*)

MAN. Add fifteen percent.

WOMAN. I'll tell him how much to add. Add twenty percent.

(*MAN gives him the check and a credit card, and WAITER exits.*)

MAN. Don't gloat.

WOMAN. Why not? I won.

MAN. You had to cheat.
WOMAN. There are no rules.
MAN. You don't really believe that.
WOMAN. I told the truth. That's the ultimate weapon.
MAN. If you call truth a weapon, you are pretty far gone.

(WAITER returns with a salver holding credit card and invoice. HE lays it beside the Man and exits.)

WOMAN. You all stick together, don't you?

(SHE takes the invoice. HE picks up the credit card off the tray and plays with it, as she bends to sign.)

MAN. Look me in the eye and tell me you're proud of what you did.
WOMAN. I am very, very proud. I thought this would be another night to forget. With another bitter, predictable prick. But I was wrong. I want to remember this. When my statement comes, I'm going to frame it and put it on my wall. Every time I look at it, I'll think of you. *(SHE signs the slip and tears off her copy.)* Could I have my card?

(HE hands it to her.)

WOMAN. So long, loser. *(SHE exits.)*

(MAN stares thoughtfully at his coffee. WAITER enters and picks up the credit card invoice.)

WAITER. Sir, there's some mix-up here. This isn't your signature.
MAN. I know.
WAITER. Your friend signed on *your* credit card?
MAN. She must have thought I gave you hers. She'll see her mistake when she gets her statement.
WAITER. Shall I run your card through again?

MAN. "There are no rules." Everybody says that. But they don't accept it. Not down deep. (*HE tears up the credit slip and hands his card to Waiter.*) And do it right this time.

WAITER. Sir?

MAN. You added twenty-five percent. After she said twenty. Make it fifteen. Exactly. Because I've got my eye on you.

(Curtain.)

THE END

THE INTERROGATION
A Comedy in One Scene

by Murphy Guyer

The Interrogation premiered at the Actors Theatre of Louisville on May 25, 1982. It was directed by Robert Spera and had the following cast:

MAN ....Joel Hammer
WOMAN ....Katherine Klekas

Set Design: Jonathan W. Sprouse
Lighting Design: Jonathan W. Sprouse
Costume Design: Diana S. Cain
Sound Design: Grace Bennett
Property Master: Jolene Obertin
Production Stage Manager: Corey Beth Madden

THE INTERROGATION

Winter. A bar in New York City. A table and two chairs. Seated in one of the chairs is a MAN in his late twenties. HE is attractive in a seedy, unkempt sort of way. On the table in front of him are three shot glasses; two empty, one full. Also a glass of water. On the other side of the table sits a Scotch on the rocks, untouched. In the center of the table is a large ashtray brimming with gnarled cigarette butts. The MAN is waiting. HE drums his fingers. HE looks behind him toward the door to the bar. HE checks his watch. HE downs the shot of whiskey. HE stares at the table top and is momentarily lost in distant thought. HE snaps out of it and looks toward the door again. HE grabs his pack of cigarettes and discovers that it's empty. HE removes a fresh pack from his pocket, opens it, and removes a cigarette. HE flicks his disposable lighter a number of times but gets no flame. HE shakes it and flicks again. Still nothing. HE holds it up to the light to see if it's empty. HE continues to shake and flick as a WOMAN enters behind him. SHE too is in her mid-twenties. Attractive and well dressed, SHE sports a deep tan and positively radiates good health. SHE stands and observes the Man for a moment, not dissatisfied with what she sees. The MAN brings his lighter to his nose and sniffs. The WOMAN smiles at this.

WOMAN. Hi.

MAN. ... Oh, hi.

WOMAN. Snorting butane again.

MAN. (*Smiling sheepishly.*) Out of gas.

WOMAN. Am I very late?

MAN. (*Hastening to reassure.*) No, no. Not very.

WOMAN. Trying to find a cab on Sunday is like trying to find a rabbi in Wyoming.

(MAN rises to help her off with her coat but is too late. SHE has already managed it by herself without seeming to even notice his attempt. As THEY settle into their chairs:)

MAN. So ... How are you? How ya been?

WOMAN. Can't complain. Same old table I see.

MAN. Yeah, same old spot ... You look good.

WOMAN. Thanks. I feel good.

MAN. You've lost weight.

WOMAN. It's a new diet. I can eat anything I want as long as I don't swallow.

MAN. *(Laughs with solicitous appreciation.)* Where'd you get the sun?

WOMAN. St. Martin.

MAN. St. Martin.

WOMAN. It's an island in the Caribbean.

MAN. Yeah, I know. I was just ... It's Dutch, isn't it?

WOMAN. Half Dutch, half French. I was on the French side.

MAN. Terrific. Vacation?

WOMAN. Yeah. Just got back on Monday.

MAN. How was it? Have a good time?

WOMAN. It was glorious. I didn't want to leave.

MAN. And ya got a new hairstyle.

WOMAN. It's easier to manage.

MAN. *(Rummaging for matches.)* Looks good.

WOMAN. Thanks. Is this for me?

MAN. Yeah. Dewars on the rocks, right?

WOMAN. Well no, actually I don't drink anymore. Here, why don't you drink it and I'll drink your water. It *is* water isn't it?

MAN. Yeah, yeah. You don't drink anymore?

WOMAN. Too many calories.

MAN. You want a light beer? I'll go to the bar and get—

WOMAN. No, no. This is fine.

MAN. Listen, could I borrow your lighter or a match or something?

WOMAN. Sorry, I quit.

(MAN looks at her dumbfounded. HE is stunned. This is getting distressing.)

MAN. You quit smoking?

WOMAN. I had to. It was interfering with my running.

MAN. Your running?

WOMAN. I took up jogging a few months ago. I was fine for the first couple of miles but after that I just didn't have wind. So I quit smoking.

MAN. You run two miles a day?

WOMAN. Five now.

MAN. *(Incredulous.)* Five miles a *day*?

WOMAN. When I can. Depends on the weather.

MAN. *(Smiling but pained HE looks for a cloud in the silver lining of her life.)* Geez ... Must get kind of boring, huh?

WOMAN. No. Actually I find it rather exhilarating.

(MAN returns his cigarette back into the pack. After a brief, uncertain pause HE makes another effort at affability.)

MAN. So ... What did you do today?

WOMAN. Not much. Slept late. Bought a paper. Played a few games of racquetball.

MAN. Racquetball?

WOMAN. I joined a club.

MAN. *(Sinking into despair.)* ... Must be nice.

WOMAN. I enjoy it. How about you?

MAN. *(Too depressed to lie.)* I went to Burger King.

WOMAN. Sounds exciting.

MAN. Yeah, you know. Separated my hard french fries from my soft french fries, did the puzzles on my placemat,—

WOMAN. —spilled ketchup on your shirt.

MAN. What? Where?

WOMAN. Fourth button down.

MAN. ... Oh. No, that's pizza. From last night.

WOMAN. With anchovies?

MAN. As usual.

WOMAN. I'll never understand how you can eat those things. It's like eating greasy caterpillars.

MAN. I don't know. I find them rather exhilarating.

WOMAN. ... Funny.

MAN. So ... How's your love life?

WOMAN. Can't complain.

MAN. Been seeing anybody?

WOMAN. A few people.

(MAN nods agreeably. Pause.)

WOMAN. How's Maria? She still playing accordion at that restaurant?

MAN. *(Uncomfortably.)* I'm uh, not seeing Maria anymore.

WOMAN. Oh? What happened?

MAN. It just didn't work out.

WOMAN. Did she go back to Spain?

MAN. *(Looks at her, trying to ascertain if this mistake was intentional. HE can't tell.)* Portugal.

(Brief pause.)

WOMAN. So she walked out on you huh?

MAN. *(Anticipating this.)* No she didn't walk out on me. It was a mutual decision.

WOMAN. Aren't they all. When did this happen?

MAN. *(Cavalierly.)* I don't know. A month or so ago.

WOMAN. That's a shame.

(HE looks at her to determine if she is being facetious but SHE is giving nothing away. Pause.)

MAN. What about you?

WOMAN. What.

MAN. *(Matter of factly.)* Been to bed with anyone?

WOMAN. ... What kind of question is that?

MAN. I don't know. I'm curious.

WOMAN. Well I didn't take a vow of celibacy if that's what you mean.

(Pause.)

MAN. *(Even more matter of factly.)* How many?
WOMAN. What?
MAN. How many men have you slept with?
WOMAN. *(Drily sarcastic.)* I don't know. I stopped counting at thirty seven.
MAN. *(With a half-hearted chuckle.)* No, seriously.
WOMAN. I don't think that's any of your business.
MAN. Why don't you want to tell me?
WOMAN. What do you want to know for?
MAN. I'm curious that's all. It's an honest question, what's the big deal?
WOMAN. Four.

(MAN's artificial geniality melts away.)

MAN. *(Blankly.)* Four?
WOMAN. Yeah.
MAN. You gotta be kidding.
WOMAN. What's the matter with that?
MAN. Four different guys?
WOMAN. Oh knock it off. You asked me and I told you.
MAN. Jesus.
WOMAN. Jesus what?
MAN. I mean one I could understand. Two *maybe*. Even three if you were drunk, or unconscious, or—
WOMAN. *(Irked.)* Would you mind telling me what is so awful about that?
MAN. *(With facetious nonchalance.)* Nothing. It's great. Just great.
WOMAN. Nine months is a long time.
MAN. Yeah. Especially when you're bedridden.
WOMAN. You had Maria.

MAN. Yeah. *One.*

WOMAN. Well you shouldn't have limited yourself to Spanish immigrants with unnaturally large breasts.

MAN. She was Portuguese.

WOMAN. And it's none of your business what I do. You left me, remember?

MAN. Yeah, and I can see you were real broke up about it.

WOMAN. What were you expecting? A suicide attempt?

(MAN retreats. Pause.)

MAN. *(Back to his breezy manner.)* So how were they?

WOMAN. What?

MAN. These guys. How were they?

WOMAN. Oh for God's sake.

MAN. It's an honest question.

WOMAN. It's none of your business.

MAN. I'd like to know.

WOMAN. Why?

MAN. I'm curious, that's all.

WOMAN. *(Losing some of her composure.)* Well stop being curious. I don't want to talk about it.

MAN. *(Backing off.)* All right. All right.

WOMAN. Talk about something else.

MAN. Fine, fine.

WOMAN. Give me some of that Scotch.

(Impulsively SHE reaches across the table and grabs the glass of Scotch. HE watches her drink. Pause.)

MAN. So ... How long were you in St. Martin?

WOMAN. Nine days.

MAN. Did you go by yourself?

WOMAN. *(Pointedly, as if to say "don't start.")* I went with Ruthie.

MAN. *(Lifts his palms defensively. The falsely accused protesting his innocence. Pause.)* Did you go to bed with anybody while you were—

WOMAN. Jesus Christ, what is your problem?

MAN. It's an honest question.

WOMAN. I'm fed up with your honest questions.

MAN. (*Generously affable.*) What's the big deal? You don't have to answer. If you don't want to answer, don't.

WOMAN. Thanks. I won't.

MAN. (*Slamming his fist on the table.*) I knew it.

WOMAN. Oh my God.

MAN. You did, didn't you.

WOMAN. I don't believe this.

MAN. Well? Didn't you?

WOMAN. Yes, I did. All right? Satisfied?

MAN. Were *you*?

WOMAN. Oh pa-lease.

MAN. No wonder you hated to leave.

WOMAN. Whatever you say.

MAN. Who was he? Some greasy Frog bartender with slim hips?

WOMAN. No, he was an American lifeguard with broad shoulders.

MAN. (*Getting on a roll.*) A lifeguard! Well, well, how fascinating! How, how primitive! Did he walk upright?

WOMAN. He graduated Magna Cum Lauda from the University of Miami.

MAN. No! *THE* University of Miami?! Wow! Imagine that. That's a correspondence program isn't it?

WOMAN. Don't be such a snob.

MAN. What was his major? Snorkeling?

WOMAN. All right, that's enough.

MAN. Well you certainly didn't lose any time. Nine days. Jesus H—

WOMAN. One more remark like that and I'm leaving. Now knock it off.

(*MAN retreats broodingly. WOMAN glares at him. Long, tense pause. Then, just as WOMAN turns away:*)

MAN. So how was he?

WOMAN. (*Snapping with furious exasperation.*) Will you shut up?!

MAN. Fine! Fine! You don't want to talk about it? Fine!

WOMAN. I don't believe this.

MAN. I certainly wouldn't want you to betray any beautiful trust. I mean I wouldn't want you to cheapen some rare, inexpressible—

WOMAN. (*Exploding.*) HE WAS GREAT! He was incredible! He was tall and he was blonde and he had gorgeous blue eyes and rippling bronze muscles! I was drooling with desire and he knew it!

MAN. (*Glancing furtively about the bar.*) Keep your voice down will ya? There are—

WOMAN. HE KNEW IT! He played me like a Stradivarius! He swept me off my feet and carried me to the beach. He laid me in the moonlit surf and ripped off his clothes. He undressed me with his teeth and I gurgled with delight. My quivering quim yearned for his pulsating rod. I panted and I moaned and I screamed dirty words. We thrashed about like two sex-starved beasts. He ravished me again and again. I begged for him to stop but he only laughed. Finally, with dawn breaking on the horizon, and waves crashing against my trembling thighs, I fainted out of sheer ecstasy!

(*WOMAN sits and crosses her arms with finality. MAN stares off in mortified resentment. Pause. MAN looks down at the floor, struggling against the compulsion welling up inside of him. Ultimately though, the compulsion wins and:*)

MAN. Did you have an orgasm?

WOMAN. Dear God. You are being ridiculous!

MAN. (*Bursting with furious self-loathing.*) OF COURSE I'M BEING RIDICULOUS! YOU THINK I DON'T KNOW I'M BEING RIDICULOUS?! YOU THINK I *LIKE* BEING RIDICULOUS?! ... Give me some of that water.

(MAN reaches across the table and snatches the glass of water. HE gulps it down feverishly. HE holds the cool glass against his forehead. The WOMAN watches him with bemused indulgence. Pause.)

WOMAN. Who cut your hair?
MAN. Guy around the corner.
WOMAN. Very creative.
MAN. He was cheap.
WOMAN. Any scars?

(HE raises his head and gives her a "gimme-a-break" look.)

WOMAN. *(Drily.)* You look like shit.
MAN. Well we can't all look like a "Come-to-Jamaica" poster.
WOMAN. *(Laughs in spite of herself.)* I do look pretty plastic, don't I.
MAN. No you don't. You look great. It's depressing.

(Pause.)

WOMAN. *(Serious.)* You hurt me you know.
MAN. *(Wracked with guilt.)* I know ... I know, I'm sorry.
WOMAN. I wanted to punch your teeth out.
MAN. I don't blame you.
WOMAN. I had all these elaborate fantasies about how I was going to get back at you. I was going to send you a dead rat through the mail. Get some guy with an Italian accent to leave menacing messages on your answering machine.
MAN. Why didn't you?
WOMAN. I didn't want to give you the satisfaction.
MAN. I missed you.
WOMAN. How could you do it?
MAN. *(Grasping helplessly.)* ... I don't know. I was ... It was a mistake.
WOMAN. You bastard.
MAN. I still love you.

(Getting emotional in spite of herself, the WOMAN grows frantic. The following exchange should accelerate and grow in intensity as the WOMAN searches about distractedly while MAN presses with needy solicitousness.)

WOMAN. Oh Christ, why did I come here.
MAN. You want to leave?
WOMAN. I hate this place.
MAN. You want to go someplace else?
WOMAN. They haven't changed the jukebox in thirty years.
MAN. Are you tired?
WOMAN. *Or* the sawdust on the floor.
MAN. You want to sleep with me?
WOMAN. *(Without hesitation.)* Yes.

(HE kisses her impulsively. It lasts. THEY look at each other with undisguised need.)

MAN. *(Suddenly.)* Let's get out of here.

(THEY begin throwing on their coats and scarfs with great urgency.)

WOMAN. I must be out of my mind.
MAN. Hey, we can pick up some ice cream on the way.
WOMAN. Where's my scarf? Where's my scarf?
MAN. It's around your neck.
WOMAN. Oh. Ice cream. Great. There goes my diet.
MAN. *(Counting out crumpled dollar bills.)* Then we won't get any.
WOMAN. Yes we will. And I want mocha mint chip. *(SHE starts off.)*
MAN. Oh listen, I meant to ask you something.

(SHE stops at the exit as HE tosses the bills on the table.)

MAN. That lifeguard. Was he number five or was he included in the four?

WOMAN. Oh Christ. (*SHE exits exhaustedly.*)

MAN. (*As HE hurries after her.*) What? What's wrong? It's an honest question.

BLACKOUT

THE END

SCRUPLES

by
Jon Jory

Scruples premiered at the Actors Theatre of Louisville on December 11, 1989. It was directed by Bob Krakower and had the following cast:

LOIS	Diane Casey
JANE	Belinda Morgan
MARTI	Marta Johnson
MRS. DOBBS	Connan Morrissey
MR. SKILES	Bruce Romans

Production Manager: Bob Krakower
Sound Designer: Mark Hendren
Scenic Designer: Paul Owen
Property Master: Mark Bissonnette
Costume Designer: Melissa Pepper
Lighting Designer: David P. Misern
Stage Managers: Mary Czoolgosz, Karen Price, Hannah Vesenka
Dramaturg: Carrie Luft

TIME & PLACE

The present. A waiting room.

SCRUPLES

FOUR WOMEN sit in a "waiting" room. Silence.
THEY smile nervously at each other. THEY look away.
Pause.

LOIS. (*Throws a fit in a minor way.*) Aaaaaarrrrgggh!

(THEY look at her, startled.)

LOIS. Just thought I'd admit the tension. Anybody want licorice?
JANE. No, thanks.
MARTI. (*Indecisive.*) Ummmm.
LOIS. (*Handing it over.*) Take it.
MARTI. (*Regards it as if it were from outer space.*) Ummmm.
LOIS. You'll have to pull some off yourself; I don't like to touch it. Don't you hate to think about how they keep this stuff soft? Think about ingesting chemicals that keep things limp indefinitely. Brrrrr.

(MARTI hands it back to her without eating any.)

LOIS. Listen, what are we doing here?
MARTI. Doing? (*Pause.*) Here?
JANE. In the larger sense, or the smaller sense?
LOIS. In the smaller sense.
JANE. We're auditioning for a Nightsilk commercial.
MARTI. Yeah!
LOIS. (*Regards Marti a moment, and then speaks to Jane.*) Well, you've identified my problem; what's Nightsilk?
JANE. (*Deadpan—Unsmiling—Quoting.*) Pantyhose, with the elegant sheen of the autumn moon on glass-smooth water. Pantyhose so luxurious, so limpid, so delicately sensual you will

experience across the centuries the serene confidence of the Chinese empresses.

(A pause.)

MARTI. *(Sincerely.)* That was *so* good.

(A pause.)

LOIS. Jesus!
MARTI. *(Startled.)* What?
LOIS. It's worse than I thought.
JANE. *(Infinitesimally defensive.)* What's worse?
LOIS. Having principles. Having principles is worse.
JANE. You dropped your licorice.
LOIS. See, I dropped my licorice. Great. I dropped my licorice. Wonderful. *(To Jane.)* Would you mind telling me if you're an idealist?
JANE. No, I'm not an idealist.
LOIS. I wanted to eat this licorice.

(Pause.)

MARTI. I'm an idealist.
LOIS. You're an idealist?
MARTI. Ummmmm.
LOIS. In what sense?
MARTI. In what sense?
LOIS. *(Carefully.)* In what sense are you an idealist?
MARTI. *(Pause.)* Sort of in the sense of hoping for the best.
LOIS. In art?
MARTI. In art?
LOIS. In art, in art.
MARTI. Oh, art.

(A pause.)

LOIS. (*Tense.*) Do you hope for the best in art?

JANE. Excuse me. When I go up for a commercial, I have to face the fact I am one of several hundred women competing for the attention of a casting agent with the I.Q. of a chimpanzee and the hostility of a King Cobra. In that situation it's really a lot better to be calm and centered if you know what I mean, and I find that silence is a real help.

LOIS. Really?

JANE. Yes.

LOIS. Wow. (*A pause.*) I find it's such a dehumanizing process that making contact with the other women gives me a perspective that allows me to go on living. (*Pause.*) So I like to talk.

MARTI. See, I feel you both have better legs.

(*A pause.*)

LOIS. Goddammit!

MARTI. What?

LOIS. I don't think we should talk about it.

(*A pause.*)

JANE. (*Against her better judgment.*) What?

LOIS. I really shouldn't start. (*A pause—to Jane.*) Do you really want to know?

(*A pause.*)

JANE. Moderately.

(*A pause.*)

LOIS. All right. (*A pause—when she starts, SHE goes* very *fast.*) First of all, I'm an actress. An actress. I am personally committed to holding a mirror up to nature. To show not only what *is* but what *can be.* To say *yes* to life. To illuminate the soul, penetrate literature, and apply the electric shock of truth to a society which is practically moribund and so confused it celebrates form over content and acquisition instead of perception. So, auditioning for a commercial is betrayal on the deepest level of the very vocation I've made central to my existence, but let's not worry about *that*!

JANE. Okay.

LOIS. Let's look at it on a societal basis. Let's take it in terms of images internalized by millions of viewers which provide the raw material for their attitudes *toward* and misconceptions *of* women.

JANE. Maybe I'll have a piece of licorice.

LOIS. (*Tearing a strip off and handing it to her while she talks.*) Women are smooth, women are silky, women are meant to be touched. The most important part of women is below the waist, and all, all of this can be enhanced or possessed for less than three dollars a pair. So that both as an artist and a woman I am actively involved in demeaning what, up to this point, I have proudly defined as my ideals, my talent, myself, and my body. Is that clear?

JANE. I think I took it in.

MARTI. But you really do have good legs, though.

JANE. I have a very big phone bill. All the people I ever liked now live in Seattle. I am way behind on my rent on a recently remodeled two-level linen closet on the upper west side which is about to go condo. I support my boyfriend who has trained for ten years for a classical theatre which does not exist, and, currently, the only food in my place is a case of Golden Grahams Crunchy Wheat and Marshmallow breakfast cereal which I won in a telephone promotion. It is perfectly all right with me if they show pictures of my legs on television, because it is the truth that I *have* legs and, thus, showing them *is* holding the mirror up to nature.

LOIS. (*Gently.*) You have a slave mentality.

MARTI. Do we have to say lines?

JANE. Lines?

MARTI. I've been a hand and foot model for six years. My dream is to say lines.

(Pause.)

JANE. I think it's legs and a voice-over.
MARTI. Oh.

(Pause.)

JANE. *(Needled.)* For thousands of years people earned their bread by having A) strong arms, B) a strong back, C) strong legs. Just because men view legs as hors d'oeuvres is no reason I have to hide the fact I'm healthy. Plus, lest we forget, truth and beauty. I quote Keats, or somebody, "Beauty is truth, truth beauty. That is all you know on earth, and all you need to know," or something. I am here defending Beauty, the ideal. To say someone has beautiful legs, you must first idealize the leg, then you judge the leg against the ideal, and the one that comes closest gets the commercial. To the irate feminist I say beauty transcends oppression. The answer to your other question is, they keep licorice soft with a chemical called antiocasnibromizine, which is a carcinogen that will eventually melt your intestines and kill you.

(Pause.)

MARTI. I think silence is the greatest sin. I feel so much, but I can't say it. It would be a great step forward for me to speak in front of people on television.

(Pause.)

LOIS. Is Nightsilk pantyhose a good product?
JANE. I don't know.
LOIS. Is it ever right to compromise your ideals for money?
JANE. Yes.
LOIS. I think it's pretty clear that my legs are better than yours, so if I stay here I will get the commercial and you won't.
JANE. In that case, it is wrong to compromise your ideals for money.
LOIS. I'm very close to getting a good role in a Spanish movie

about transcending gender in politics that means a great deal to me, but they want to see film on me, any kind of film, so I came here thinking it would be all right to compromise my principles so that I could act on them later.

JANE. You're a very confused person, Lois.

MARTI. My dad raced stock cars, and he used to say that once you got over 130 miles an hour the most dangerous thing to your health was thinking.

(A pause—an efficient WOMAN in a suit enters.)

MRS. DOBBS. *(Pleasant, straight-forward and without artifice.)* Good morning.

LOIS. Good morning.

JANE. Good morning.

(THEY all look at Marti. SHE waves.)

MRS. DOBBS. I am glad to see you, Lois, Jane and Marti. I am Letitia Dobbs.

JANE. Hello, Mrs. Dobbs.

LOIS. Hello, Letitia.

MARTI. *(A pause.)* Hi.

MRS. DOBBS. I handle East Coast casting for Nightsilk pantyhose. The three of you, selected from hundreds of young women, are our final callbacks not for simply *a* commercial but for a series of commercials filmed over a two-year period, which the winner will find very, very, very, very, very, very lucrative. Nightsilk, realizing that its products could be categorized as trivial and cognizant that unpopular animal research is crucial to developing world-class pantyhose is donating two cents a pair to African famine relief, which on our annual sales of over a billion dollars will provide over two million dollars of food supplies, so you will be not only body parts but spokespersons and benefactors. Thus, while only your legs will be filmed, we will be wanting you to do a good deal of speaking and traveling on our behalf. Please remember also that legs are not simply sculptural, not simply matter. There are millions of technically attractive legs, but they can be more, much more. Legs can be infused with a sense of self and spirit which animates them on camera and communicates to the viewer with damaged self-esteem new goals and new hope. A beautiful soul makes beautiful legs, and Nightsilk, by enhancing the leg, enhances the soul.

(JANE applauds.)

MRS. DOBBS. Thank you. We are, mincing no words, looking for an uncommon woman for an uncommon job in uncommon times. The callback will begin with a forty-minute in-depth interview exploring your world view and your attitudes toward both our project and our product. Then, of course, in a monitored environment we will be asking you to take off your clothes. Please relax and center yourself for this exciting and challenging process. My assistant, Mr. Skiles will be around shortly with fruit frappes and nibbles. Nightsilk pantyhose apologizes that we are running ... *(Checks her watch.)* forty minutes behind schedule, we know your time is valuable. I can tell by speaking with you that you are lovely and intelligent young women with caring and remarkable parents. Are there any questions?

(Pause.)

MARTI. Is there a ladies' room?
MRS. DOBBS. *(Pleasant as always.)* No, I'm afraid not. *(To all of them.)* Good luck. *(SHE exits.)*

(A pause.)

LOIS. *(In complete moral conflict.)* Dammit!! *(SHE gets up, starts to leave, stops, returns and sits down.)*

(Tears run down MARTI's face.)

JANE. *(To Marti.)* It's okay. You'll do fine.

(A good-looking young MAN in a suit enters with a brightly colored plastic tray with coffee, cups, sugar and cream. HE stops.)

MR. SKILES. Hey, babes. I'm Ricky Skiles, Mrs. Dobbs' lackey and designated fantasy sex object. Any of you gorgeous gams looking for a hit of caffeine?

LIGHTS OUT

THE END

The Man Who Couldn't Dance

by
Jason Katims

THE MAN WHO COULDN'T DANCE

The attic of Gail's house in Connecticut. ELIZABETH sleeps in her crib. ERIC and GAIL enter.

GAIL. Not too loud.

(THEY walk to crib. Look in.)

GAIL. Eric, this is Elizabeth.
ERIC. Oh my God. She's really ... ugly.
GAIL. What?
ERIC. The kid is like a raisin or something.
GAIL. *(To Elizabeth, whispering.)* Don't listen to him Elizabeth. He's jealous. *(To Eric.)* I've been wanting so much for you to meet her. It's like it would make the whole thing real or something.
ERIC. God. She's a beautiful little raisin, isn't she? It's what was behind door number two.
GAIL. What?
ERIC. I don't know. All night I haven't been able to shake this feeling. It's like I'm visiting the life I could have had. A baby. A house in Connecticut. A subscription to *House and Garden*.
GAIL. You won't let me outlive that one will you?
ERIC. Come on Gail. *House and Garden*.
GAIL. I put it in the basket in the bathroom for *you*, you know. I remember how frightened you used to be of bathrooms without reading material.
ERIC. Don't make me into some sort of like neurotic old boyfriend Gail.
GAIL. Are you going to deny your severe fear of bathrooms?
ERIC. Bathrooms are frightening, horrible places. Cold. Lonely. Sterile. But you should not use that to make me into some kind of little anecdote. Like a chapter of your life that was some

little situation comedy. Do not mistake neurotic fears and obsessions for light comedy. Very dangerous, Gail.

GAIL. I don't want to get into a discussion like this now, Eric.

ERIC. What kind of discussion is it, and when *would* you like to get into it?

GAIL. A discussion about us. And never. They're waiting.

ERIC. They're fine on their own.

GAIL. What is that supposed to mean?

ERIC. What?

GAIL. They're *fine* on their own. *Fine?*

ERIC. It doesn't mean anything.

GAIL. Are you saying that my husband is attracted to your girl friend. Is that it?

ERIC. Wooo. Hold on Gail. All I said was they're fine on their own.

GAIL. Fred and I happen to be very, very happy. Together. He's not interested in some twenty-three-year-old music student and her stupid thesis on Todd Rundgren.

ERIC. You seemed very interested over dinner.

GAIL. Who the hell would write a thesis on Todd Rundgren? Is she going to hand out T-shirts and loose joints at her orals?

ERIC. She's just a date, Gail. A date.

GAIL. It didn't sound like that on the phone. "She's beautiful. She's intelligent. She's not hung up by society's rules." These are your words. I think you should grow up.

ERIC. Why?

GAIL. Why should you grow up? Are you asking me why you should grow up?

ERIC. Yes. I'm interested in hearing about it from someone who thinks she has.

GAIL. That is what people do. They get married. They have kids. They remember their ideals fondly. They try to stick to them in their own way. They donate to public television. They get by.

ERIC. Don't cry, Gail. Please do not cry.

GAIL. Oooh that gets me. What makes you think I'm going to cry?

ERIC. Because you regret your choices. And now you're going

to cry.

GAIL. I regret my choices? Fuck you.

ERIC. I'm sorry. I said what I thought. I broke the unwritten rule between us since we broke up. I'm supposed to smile, and talk to you like I'm really interested in just the right amount of sugar to put into the pecan pie recipe.

GAIL. I can't believe you said that thing about *my* pie.

ERIC. I liked the pie. I thought it had a little too much sugar. I just don't understand why everyone who makes pecan pie is obligated to put too much sugar in it because every other pecan pie has too much sugar in it. It's like a world doomed to repeat its horrors. I eat that pecan pie and I think we're just marking time until the next goddamn Holocaust.

GAIL. Are you saying I baked a Nazi pie?

ERIC. Not intentionally.

GAIL. You shouldn't have criticized my pie in front of company.

ERIC. Gail, I am the company.

(A beat.)

GAIL. Oh am I glad that you are not the father of my daughter. I am so happy to not have to worry for her about your inconsistency, your stubbornness, your uncanny ability to make the most politically and philosophically interesting choices leaving yourself and your loved ones in the shit heap. Let's just spend the rest of the night playing Pictionary. All right?

ERIC. This is the fourth time tonight you brought up Pictionary. Are you forcing me to play fucking Pictionary?

GAIL. It's just a game, Eric. Or am I wrong. Is it actually going to join forces with pecan pie to cause the next Holocaust?

ERIC. It's a waste of time. People sit around and solve meaningless little puzzles and form arbitrary alliances for no other reason than to pass time. Well, time is passing well enough for me without games, Gail. Fred wastes enough of my time talking about his fucking boat. Does he really think I care about his fucking boat? All right, great. He bought a motorized flotation device.

Does he really think I want to go on for hour after hour about it?

GAIL. So good. It's good to know how you feel about Fred.

ERIC. How do I feel about Fred?

GAIL. I always knew you didn't like him.

ERIC. How can I like him or not like him? I don't know him. I know his boat. I could draw the blueprints for his fucking boat. I don't know *him*.

GAIL. It's so goddamn easy for you.

ERIC. What?

GAIL. It's so easy for you *not* to play Pictionary. You're funny, verbal, provocative. Do you know how intimidated my husband is by you?

ERIC. Play fucking Pictionary, Gail. Play your heart out. I'll stay here with Elizabeth.

GAIL. You belong with Elizabeth.

ERIC. Purity-wise?

GAIL. Maturity-wise.

ERIC. (*Change of tone.*) You don't love Fred.

GAIL. What?

ERIC. You don't love Fred.

GAIL. That's it. I demand that you play Pictionary, Eric. I goddamn insist.

ERIC. Why did you marry a man you didn't love?

GAIL. I never said I don't love him.

ERIC. Christ, Gail. Tell me you love him. Please.

GAIL. YOU GOT ON THAT FUCKING BOAT. The crucial point. The pinnacle time. The absolute quintessential turning point of our relationship and you're on a fucking boat to fucking Saint John.

ERIC. That has nothing to do with it.

GAIL. It's got everything to do with it.

ERIC. You make it sound like you made some kind of choice between two men. Like it was me or him.

GAIL. It was.

ERIC. It was? Come on Gail. It's a huge world. If it were a choice between me or Fred most women would just fucking shoot themselves.

GAIL. You threw it away.

ERIC. I never threw you away.

GAIL. Not *me*. It. Everything. Eric you're such an asshole. Everyone's goddamn guru. Living by your values. True to yourself. The ascetic. The 20th Century Philosopher. Eric, I have a question for you. A real question. Why are you working on a farm? Why? It's like I'm supposed to admire you or something. I'm so sick of your untraditional paths. The Farm Boy from Bensonhurst. You're wasting your intelligence. You're wasting your intelligence to pick vegetables. There is nothing to admire about that. It's stupid.

ERIC. You're right. Why work with my hands to produce a reasonably priced source of nourishment for my fellow human beings while I could be getting fat and playing Pictionary.

GAIL. I gained four pounds. *Four*. Don't you dare say I'm getting fat. And there is nothing wrong with playing Pictionary, you goddamn all-knowing fool. You lost me.

ERIC. I know.

GAIL. It pisses me off. It really pisses me off. That thing you said about me regretting my choices. At least I made a choice.

ERIC. But you do regret it.

GAIL. I love Fred, Eric. I do love him. Not like I loved you. But we have these things together. This family. This feeling. This sureness.

ERIC. I don't consider your need for structure your strongest trait.

GAIL. Look, Eric, I don't think I can have this conversation with you. I'm sorry things had to happen the way they happened. Let's go downstairs.

ERIC. Right. I'm sorry.

GAIL. You're just being yourself.

ERIC. That's what I'm sorry for. I should say goodbye to Elizabeth. Who knows when I'll see her again.

(ERIC walks to the crib. HE looks down. In a moment HE bends over to her.)

GAIL. Eric! She'll wake up.

(But ERIC lifts her into his arms. When HE turns back his face is flush with TEARS.)

GAIL. Eric. What is it?

(ERIC coddles Elizabeth. HE puts his lips to her forehead. HE places her gently back in the crib.)

GAIL. What?

ERIC. It's um. It's this thing I need to tell you. I can't dance, Gail.

GAIL. You can't dance. This is why you're crying? Eric, a lot of people can't dance.

ERIC. I don't know why I can't dance. But it's—I can't. I can't make my body move in these ways that the music is demanding that I move. It's just so goddamn embarrassing. The situation. I mean, standing in public around hundreds of people who are displaying their purist, truest selves. I mean, it takes them no more than two drinks and their souls are out there on the dance floor. Their goodness. Their sensuality. They're sharing and loving. I watch that, look at that. But my body fights it. I start to analyze the music. The rhythm. The time signature. I understand the theory of dancing. The *idea* of spontaneously sharing in this moment that exists now and only now. The give and take with your partner. Two mirrors on a land where gravity holds you to this point and then leaves you free. And that the universe happens right there and then. Like, truth. I understand this intellectually. But Gail, I never have experienced it. I can't dance.

GAIL. How did Elizabeth make you think of that?

ERIC. When we were together. There were all these times when you would arrange for us to be in these places. These parties. And invariably there would be a band, or music playing and invariably people would start dancing.

GAIL. I would arrange this? Like I did this to you?

ERIC. Invariably you would want to dance. And I wouldn't dance with you. I wouldn't dance with you, Gail. And I could see the hurt register on your face. I could see the anger build within you. I could see that this just wouldn't do for you.

GAIL. Why didn't you just say I can't dance. Why didn't you just tell me?

ERIC. Because it was the dam holding the water. If I let that out. That one thing, everything would follow. I couldn't dance. I couldn't have a normal talk about the weather with a neighbor without getting into a conversation about God, love and eternity. I mean, after all, the weather has these huge connotations. I couldn't act correctly in social situations. I couldn't sacrifice truth for a relationship. I couldn't hold you when you needed to be held because I wanted you to be stronger. Because I wanted to be stronger. I couldn't ask you for the warmth of your touch out of need. I couldn't let myself. I would only ask for your touch out of strength. Out of something that wouldn't become sick and interdependent and symbiotic. I wasn't able to do these things. I don't know, Gail. I mean, you marrying Fred didn't really say anything to me. It was like something in this continuum. This cycle. I mean, it was this thing that happened in my life. The love of my life got married to another man. It didn't seem permanent. But the fact that Elizabeth ... The fact that this angel ... this unbelievable gift isn't mine. And will never be mine. This is killing me.

GAIL. Oh my God, Eric. You're human.

ERIC. I'll never have a daughter, Gail.

GAIL. Yes, you will.

ERIC. I'm thirty-seven. I have done nothing but make myself more isolated, unavailable, and unappealing. Believe it or not, it's difficult picking up women with this type of conversation. I work for four dollars an hour, Gail. I never earned a college degree. I can't bring myself to work for someone who is not producing something with some kind of goodness. That rules out ninety-eight percent of job openings. And the other two percent pay approximately four dollars an hour. I am not really going to change. I don't know why this is. People think I make these choices. But you've got to believe me, Gail, I have no control. I can't dance.

GAIL. I never knew you *couldn't* dance. I always thought it was that you *wouldn't* dance.

ERIC. Could you hold me?

GAIL. I don't think so, Eric. I mean, I don't think I would be able to let go.

ERIC. Yeah. You're right. (*Pause. ERIC wipes his eyes.*) Gail, there were these things that you needed. Just to breathe you needed them. And it was so clear that there was no way I was going to provide you with them. And it was this thing that I did. This thing that I did. It wasn't that horrible. You needed to find someone. I felt that you needed me off the continent. Please believe me, Gail. When I got on that boat. I was thinking of you. Not of me.

GAIL. I believe you.

ERIC. Well, this is a sign of times to come. The first time we had a conversation where your eyes stayed dry and mine didn't.

GAIL. I cried.

ERIC. We better get downstairs before Marie tells Fred about her orgy with the British invasion.

GAIL. There was one time you danced with me.

ERIC. I don't remember.

GAIL. On my wedding day.

ERIC. I couldn't have.

GAIL. You did. I remember it clearly. I remember thinking how strange it was to be in this wedding gown. On my wedding day. Dancing with you. And you weren't my groom.

ERIC. Oh yeah. That. I wasn't dancing, Gail. I was walking. I convinced myself that I was walking very slowly and sideways. It was the only way I could do it.

GAIL. Eric, maybe one day …

ERIC. Please don't say it.

GAIL. Right.

ERIC. Gail, I cannot stand Marie. I can't stand her. Please, find something to say to her about me so she won't expect me to sleep with her tonight.

GAIL. I'm sure you'll do just fine on your own.

ERIC. She was just an excuse to see you. I figured, I'd call with this woman in my life. I'd be less of a threat to the home. It was really stupid of me.

GAIL. No. It was human.

ERIC. Thank you for showing me your daughter. She is absolutely the single, greatest thing I've ever looked at in my entire life.

(THEY are about to leave.)

GAIL. Eric.

(ERIC turns. GAIL walks up to him slowly. SHE puts her head into his chest. His arms fold around her.)

GAIL. Eric, you are Fred Astaire. You are Fred Astaire.

ERIC. No, no. Sweetheart. I'm Eric.

GAIL. You are Fred Astaire. Just move the slightest bit. You have nothing to prove to anyone. Just move a little slowly. The slightest bit. Don't worry.

ERIC. We should go down there.

GAIL. In a minute. Just one minute.

(GAIL rocks back and forth musically. ERIC makes a slight movement trying to follow her. In a moment, HE relaxes. HE is dancing. GAIL reaches over, still holding him and pulls the light cord.
BLACKOUT.)

THE END

MIXED EMOTIONS

by
Bob Krakower

Mixed Emotions premiered at the Actors Theatre of Louisville on June 11, 1990. It was directed by Bob Krakower and had the following cast:

LEX...Margaret Howard
ED...Matt Kozlowski
MICHAEL ....Steve Bova
JACK..Chris Eigeman
MOIRA ....Belinda Morgan

Scenic Designer: Paul Owen
Lighting Designer: Jan Thornsberry
Costume Designer: Kevin McLeod
Sound Designer: Mark Hendren
Property Master: Mark Bissonnette
Production Manager: Bob Krakower
Stage Manager: Hannah Vesenka
Dramaturg: Kathleen Chopin

CHARACTERS

ED—He loves Lex. Just visiting ... maybe.
MICHAEL—He loves Lex. And he lives here.
MOIRA—Lex's roommate. Having an affair with Jack.
JACK—In love with Linda, but he's married. Ed's closest friend.
LEX (short for Alexa)—Spent last night with Ed. Moving in with
  Michael.

TIME & PLACE

Day. Outside. In front of the office of the Mission Rock Cafe.

MIXED EMOTIONS

LEX—pacing in front of a bench.
MICHAEL enters. Carrying duffle bags, etc.

MICHAEL. (*As HE enters, to Jack offstage.*) I'm just going up to the office to get something. Hey, Lex.
LEX. Hey, Michael.
MICHAEL. Shit, I don't have my keys. Jack?

(ED enters.)

LEX. Hi.
ED. Hi. You're here.
MICHAEL. Jack …?
LEX. I have, ya know, the thing—
MICHAEL. … you got your office keys?
ED. The *thing*. The meeting. Right, well. Good. Well, um, can I talk to you?
LEX. About what?

(JACK enters, with bags, etc.)

MICHAEL. You got your keys to the—just ah, put those down for a minute and then we'll move them to the van. Hey, Lex. (*HE kisses her on the cheek.*)
LEX. Hi.
JACK. I don't have 'em on me. They're back in the car. (*To Ed.*) Great!!! You're here already. Have a good time? Take one of these, Michael.
LEX. Have a good time doing what?
ED. I was hoping I'd see you here.
LEX. Oh. (*Pause.*) I wanted to see you, too.
MICHAEL. (*Hugs them both.*) And I wanted to see the both of

169

you.

JACK. Let's keep moving these in the van Michael, the keys are back in the car.

MICHAEL. Yeah, but ...

JACK. How are you this morning, Lex?

LEX. I'd say very, *very* good, Jack. Thank you.

JACK. This is good.

MICHAEL. (*To Ed.*) You and Lex have a good dinner last night?

JACK. Michael, can we just ...

ED. Huh? Oh, yes. Thank you.

MICHAEL. Michaelangelo's, man, best Italian in town. Worth coming back for, huh?

ED. There's a lot worth coming back for.

JACK. Let's just take these and then come back, Michael, just keep moving and then—

MICHAEL. Ya know, Eddie, there's something I wanna tell ya.

JACK. Michael, can you tell him on the way to the airport—

ED. What's up?

JACK. Michael, please.

MICHAEL. Ya know, Ed, before you came to town, Lex and I, we weren't getting along very well and—

JACK. Michael, I'll tell you what ... why don't you go back to the car and get the office keys and I'll transfer these to the van—

LEX. What he's saying is we'll be sorry to see you go.

ED. I was thinking just this morning that I really didn't *wanna* go.

(*MOIRA enters.*)

MOIRA. Ready to go?

MICHAEL. Hey, Moira.

MOIRA. Hi.

LEX. Hey, Moira.

MOIRA. Lex. I thought you said—

LEX. I lied.

JACK. You look terrific, Moira.

MICHAEL. You know Eddie, now that we're all here, I just, well, I wanted to tell ya because I don't think anybody really has, how great it's been to have you here.

ED. It's been great to be here.

MICHAEL. Lex and I were talking yesterday—

LEX. Michael.

MICHAEL. You said we oughta thank him.

LEX. I didn't mean now.

ED. Thank me?

LEX. Nothing, really.

MICHAEL. Nothing? You said if it wasn't for Eddie, we ...

JACK. ...and I'm sure that Eddie here feels good about it because as we all know Michael, if he can bring a little happiness to one person, each and every day of their life, here on earth, then he knows, that his time, is well spent. Now, can we get this kind man to his plane on time? Come, let's go back to the car ...

MICHAEL. Look all I'm trying to say is ...

LEX. Michael—

MOIRA. Um, Ed, I um, have something for you. A little, well ... going away present.

ED. For me?

MICHAEL. You do?

JACK. For *him*?

MOIRA. A little something.

JACK. Why do you have a gift for him?

MICHAEL. You okay?

LEX. Why wouldn't I be?

ED. (*Pause.*) Oh. Hahaha. Thanks. I um, really needed one just like it. Thank you.

JACK. What is that?

MOIRA. An earring that I knew he was looking for.

JACK. Jewelry?

ED. I was. It is. You must be psychic or something.

LEX. Or something.

MICHAEL. Okay! Let's get the rest of the bags out of the car and—

ED. How much time have I got?

MOIRA. We got ten minutes.

MICHAEL. And why didn't we just take, ya know, *drive* the bags right up to the van?

JACK. Because my *wife* needs to keep the car to take my kids, okay—And this is the third time I'm explaining this to you—to *school*—Fuck it, can we just go back to the car and get the rest of the bags?

ED and MOIRA. Relax, Jack.

JACK. Oh that's just great. (*HE exits.*)

MICHAEL. What's the matter with him? I was just kidding. Shit, I gotta get the keys for the office. (*HE follows Jack.*)

ED. Moira, I think Jack thinks that you and I—

MOIRA. Let him.

ED. Don't you two have a meeting or something?

MOIRA. No, we cancelled it and we're *all* taking you to the airport.

ED. You're kidding.

MOIRA. No, I'm not. Won't that be fun? (*Pause.*) I think I'll join Jack at the car. Have a little chat with him and his *wife*. (*As SHE exits.*) What a happy go lucky morning this has turned out to be.

ED. So—

LEX. So—

ED. You said you had the meeting.

LEX. Everybody seems a little frazzled today.

ED. So I see.

LEX. How about they take your plane ticket and we both stay here.

ED. You read my mind.

LEX. This doesn't happen to me very often. You?

ED. Never. (*Pause.*) I was, what would you think if—I was thinking about … staying.

LEX. Staying here?

ED. Not leaving.

LEX. With me?

ED. The thing is … I've decided—yes, with you—I've decided to stay.

LEX. Oh my God.

ED. I could get a job here, ya know?

LEX. I know.

ED. And we could be together.

LEX. Ed—

ED. And Lex, there's no one in the world I'd rather be with. I mean the things you said. Last night? Are you glad you said them?

LEX. Absolutely. And I meant them.

ED. Well, I'm glad you're glad.

LEX. Well, I'm glad that you're glad that I'm glad.

ED. Well, I'm glad that you're glad that I'm glad that you're glad that I'm glad—

(LEX's laughing, THEY move toward each other as ...
MICHAEL enters.)

MICHAEL. So what else did you guys do last night?

LEX. Why don't you go up and get the ...

MICHAEL. Oh yes ... On my way. *(To Ed.)* You're gonna love this. *(HE exits.)*

ED. What did I do that he likes me so much?

LEX. What did I do that he likes *me* so much?

ED. What do you mean?

JACK. *(Enters.)* My wife says you left some stuff at the house. A shirt, and address book, something else I can't remember.

ED. *(To Lex.)* Yeah, I have a habit of doing that.

LEX. Where's Moira?

JACK. Talking to my wife.

LEX. Gee, I wonder what they're talking about, Jack? They have so much of you in common.

(MOIRA enters.)

JACK. So, Ed? When are you coming back?

ED. I was just trying to figure that out.

JACK. Well warn us next time, okay? Every time you stay with me for longer than a week, my whole life turns inside out.

MOIRA. You can stay with us.

JACK. And then you two can *share* him. Why? So then you two can both screw him?

ED. (*Sits next to Jack.*) Come on Jack! Moira—

MICHAEL. (*Enters.*) Never have so many owed so much toooooo... Never have so many loved one person so much, no that's not it. Never have so many—

ED. Nobody owes me—

MICHAEL. (*Sits next to Ed.*) Eddie, Eddie, Eddie, Eddie. Who else am I gonna find that can drink ten cups of coffee in one sitting in Clown Alley at four o'clock in the morning?

ED. (*To Lex.*) What's a matter, you don't drink coffee?

LEX. No, I'm not a *guy*.

MICHAEL. I figure if a guy like you can like a guy like me, then I must be okay.

JACK. Personally, I can't *wait* for him to get on the fucking airplane.

MICHAEL. What's a matter? Jealous?

JACK. No. You?

ED. (*Pause.*) Um—

LEX. Why don't we get the bags to the van.

JACK. Why don't I get the van and bring it around to here.

MICHAEL. Oh. I gotta get the keys back to your wife.

(*THEY exit in separate directions.*)

ED. Uh, Moira, the earring. I don't think Jack, I mean he—

MOIRA. It's good for him.

LEX. Where did you find it?

MOIRA. Where did I find it? Right where I last saw the two of you, before you had the courtesy to move into her bedroom, rolling around on the *carpet*, that's where.

ED. Moira, I know you're enjoying this, but he's like a brother and I don't want him thinking I slept with you last night.

MOIRA. Okay, okay. Too bad though, I was enjoying this immensely. His behavior is always much better when you're around. He drinks too much, he smokes too much, and he's way too married the rest of the time. Why don't you hang around?

ED. Well, we were just talking about that.

MOIRA. (*To Lex.*) And what had we decided?

LEX. Nothing. Nothing's been decided.

(Pause.)

MOIRA. Well folks, it seems somebody better decide something, for the clock is ticking.

LEX. It's been decided. It just hasn't been discussed.

MOIRA. Well. (*Pause.*) At this point I think I'll stay in town and let you boys ride out to the airport alone together. It appeals to my sense of irony.

ED. Moira—

MOIRA. I'll go head Jack off at the van. (*SHE exits.*)

ED. I don't like missing people.

LEX. You really want to stay here?

ED. Yes, I really do. Do you want me to?

MICHAEL. (*Enters.*) Jack back? Where's Moira?

LEX. Doing what clandestine lovers do.

MICHAEL. Well, we'll do this without them, then. Ya know Eddie, without you, our little budding bistro by the bay would be most certainly ... bye-bye! Nice alliteration, huh? So, on behalf of ... all the rappin' rockers at the Mission Rock Cafe, we want to thank you for taking us from red to black and we want to make you an honorary "rocker on a mission." And with this jacket ... (*Gives jacket with name on it.*)

ED. I—gee Michael. I—

LEX. Don't feel bad. Go ahead.

MICHAEL. Wear it in good health my man. I love you. (*Gives him a hug.*) Okay. Here we go. Grab a bag, Lex.

LEX. I'm not coming.

MICHAEL. Why not?

LEX. I've got stuff to do.

MICHAEL. It won't take that long.

LEX. I'll say goodbye here.

MICHAEL. (*Pause.*) Why do you need to do that?

LEX. I'll see you over at your place in an hour.
MICHAEL. You can talk to him on the way.
LEX. I just wanna talk to him alone for a minute.
MICHAEL. (*Pause.*) Alone.
LEX. Yes. Alone.
MICHAEL. Okay. Then. Fine. Great. I'll see you at home.

(HE exits as JACK and MOIRA enter.)

JACK. Jacket looks good on you.
ED. (*To Lex. Quoting Michael.*) I'll see you at *home*?
JACK. I'm sorry Ed, I thought you and Moira, ya know, instead of you and Lex, and I—
ED. It's okay. *Home*? Lex?
JACK. Love'll do that to ya. It's wacky. Huh, Moira?

(Pause.)

MOIRA. I hope we'll see you soon, Eddie. I'll miss you. (*SHE hugs him.*) Um, let's go, Jack.
ED. Thank, Moira.

(JACK and MOIRA exit.)

LEX. Well.

(Pause.)

ED. Something you wanna tell me?
LEX. I—you and I—you're not gonna be here, okay? You don't *live* here. You understand? He loves me and he lives here and—
ED. But I'm gonna stay!!
LEX. It's a fantasy, Ed. And stranger than that, if it wasn't for you—
ED. And this is why he wanted to thank me? Why he really wanted to thank me?

LEX. Yes it is. *You don't live here!* He does. Okay? You're not gonna give up a career so you can come live with me, based on a weekend—yes, a great weekend, but *just a weekend* nonetheless,— of conventional love. That's too much pressure for me, way too much pressure. And I can't live like that. And neither can you. It's totally, totally, *totally* unrealistic, Ed.

ED. (*Pause.*) Unrealistic.

MICHAEL. (*Offstage.*) Eddie, Eddie, Eddie—You coming or going?

ED. (*Long pause.*) I guess, um, I gotta ... I'd better get going.

LEX. Yeah.

ED. I'll see you again.

LEX. Or you won't.

MICHAEL. Let's go!!!

LEX. Take care.

ED. You, too.

LEX. I do love you, ya know.

ED. Yeah. I love you, too.

(*HE exits. His bag is left onstage. SHE stares and crosses to it. SHE is left alone. LIGHTS fade to BLACK.*)

THE END

SUNDAY GO TO MEETIN'

by
Shirley Lauro

Sunday Go To Meetin' premiered at the Actors Theatre of Louisville on May 27, 1986. It was directed by Larry Deckel and had the following cast:

SALLY SUE JONES...Stefanie Vogel
HESTER BLOODWORTH...Anita Adsit
SARAH WARSAVSKY......................................Helen Greenberg

Set Design: John Saari
Lighting Design: Hunt Lewis
Master Electrician: Jeff Hill
Sound Design: David Strang
Property Mistress: Diann Fay
Production Stage Manager: Vera Williams
Costume Designer: Hollis Jenkins-Evans

CHARACTERS

SALLY SUE JONES—12 or 13. A country girl. Naive but inquisitive. Blond hair, long, tied back at nape of neck with her Sunday bow. Wears Sunday clothes—white or pastel, white high top shoes. She is a good girl, an old-fashioned girl.

HESTER BLOODWORTH—14 or 15. Also a country girl. Hester is the town dare-devil. Coquettish and mischievous and always getting into trouble. Also fair-haired. Dressed similarly to Sally Sue.

SARAH WARSAVSKY—16. Wears babushka on head and long dark skirt, black stockings. She looks very European, Semitic, dark. She has already been through a great deal in her young life and seems much older, much different and more worldly wise than the other girls.

Note: Several Yiddish phrases are spoken by Sarah. English translations are included for reference. In production, the actress speaks only the Yiddish words.

SUNDAY GO TO MEETIN'

*SCENE: A rural village in the midwest. 1905. Sunday morning.
Early autumn.*

*AT RISE: LIGHTS come up on a country road leading to a
Southern Baptist Church. A white picket fence lines the road
marking off the church property. In the distance we hear the
PARISHIONERS singing liltingly, slowly:*

OFFSTAGE VOICES. (*Singing.*)
"Give me that old time religion
Give me that old time religion
Give me that old time religion
It's good enough for me.
It was good enough for Brother
It was good enough for Sister
It was good enough for Mother
And it's good enough for me—"

*(Church is about to begin. As their voices drift off, SALLY SUE
enters on her way to Sunday School. SHE is 12 or 13, in her
Sunday best: long blond hair held at nape of neck with ribbon,
white or pastel dress, white high top shoes, carrying a Bible. As
SHE crosses stage, HESTER appears behind her. HESTER is a
year or so older than SALLY SUE and the village dare-devil.
SHE is dressed like SALLY SUE with her long, fair hair tied at
nape of neck with a big bow and carrying her Bible too.
HESTER has been running to catch up with SALLY SUE. SHE
has something important to tell her.)*

HESTER. Psst! Sally? Sally Sue?
SALLY. (*Stops, turns around. SHE is impressed with Hester
and a little afraid of her.*) Yes?

181

HESTER. (*Giggling, mischievous.*) Wanna go for a little walk with me? Right *now*??

SALLY. It's Sunday, Hester.

HESTER. (*Scoffs.*) Well, don't I *know* it's Sunday!? My Land!

SALLY. Well, I can't go for no walk! I'm almost late right now!

(SHE starts on her way, HESTER trailing her.)

HESTER. (*Coaxingly.*) Not even for a little bitty ole walk? (*SHE giggles to herself. SHE has a secret.*)

SALLY. (*Looking at her, curious.*) What kind of walk? I got to go to Sunday School—you do too!

HESTER. (*Growing mysterious.*) Oh, just a walk down the road, edge a town. Take about fifteen minutes is all—just see the wonders a the Lord all around to us to behold—among other things! (*SHE now starts off, leaving Sally in her wake.*)

SALLY. (*Now runs to catch up.*) What other things?

HESTER. (*Stops, looking at her; superior.*) Oh, things Billy Henderson has told me about.

SALLY. What kinda things he tell you about?

HESTER. (*Laughing.*) Oh now just look at you! Eyes about to bug out of your head with the curiosity, huh? Wanna come?

SALLY. What things has Billy Henderson told you about? Tell me, and I'll go!

HESTER. Well—you know over to the edge a town—that old warehouse place where the Wilkins' lived upstairs and stored their grain downstairs an stuff? That ole spooky ole tumbledown shacky place?

SALLY. What about it?

HESTER. (*Very nonchalantly while she drops this.*) Well, there's a pack a Jews moved in there—

SALLY. (*Astounded.*) WHAT??

HESTER. (*Still quite casual.*) Mmm. Opened up a fruit stand out front Billy says.

SALLY. (*Can't believe this.*) JEWS??

HESTER. Mmm. Two, three families of 'em—all related—all

lookin' jist alike Billy says. See, they bought the place and is movin' in here! *PERMANENT*!

SALLY. *HERE*??

HESTER. Mmm. They went right on down to Hawkins Law Office and Real Estate and plunked hundreds and hundreds a dollars down *cash*! Mr. Hawkins said he couldn't hardly believe his eyes how their menfolks just kept pullin' all this money outta their coat pockets and seams a their coats and jist paid for the whole place right there on the spot!

SALLY. (*Bowled over.*) No!

HESTER. It's the Lord's truth! See, Billy was jist hangin' around that ole law office and Hawkins came out and told him the whole thing—and then Billy ran on down the road and caught up to 'em and *TALKED* to 'em!

SALLY. Oh Pshaw! What'd they say?

HESTER. Nothin' much Billy could understand—jist talkin' all this foreign jibberty jaw! But Ole Man Hawkins tole Billy they come off a freighter boat from Europe. Landed on the Gulf, then moved on up from New Orleans.

SALLY. Oh my Stars! *LIVE JEWS*?!?! What'd they *look* like? Billy say?

HESTER. Didn't say too much. Funny lookin' though —not nothin' like white folks, now that's a fact.

SALLY. Crime in It'ly! I can't hardly believe it—JEWS!!

HESTER. They're sellin' apples out in front a the place Billy said. Got a wagon full of 'em parked on the road. Windfall.

SALLY. Windfall?

HESTER. Ummm—See their menfolks took this wagon and went on out to the country—Dabny's farm—and just went right onto his land and picked up the windfall apples outta his orchard, from the ground. And then went on and done the same thing at the Johnson place. And now they're sellin' 'em off, Billy says. Right now. Today.

SALLY. Sunday?

HESTER. Well, they're *Heathens,* Sally Sue. Shoot girl! Don't you know nothin'? It don't mean nothin' to *them* workin' on the Lord's Day—hey—you got any money?

SALLY. Jist my Donation is all.

HESTER. Well, I got six cents —wonder how many a them windfall apples that'd buy?

SALLY. I don't know and I don't care! I got to go—

(SHE starts off, HESTER comes after her.)

HESTER. Aw, come on—walk on over there with me—it'd jist take ten minutes—and we could sneak on into church—nobody'd see us or nothin'—Sally Sue? Come on go see—shoot! (*SHE stands in front of Sally, taking her hand.*)

SALLY. No! I'd just be too scared, Hester! Now let me pass.

(SHE pushes by HESTER who trails her again.)

HESTER. Don't have to be scared! We don't have to go inside no place or nothin'. Billy says the apples is by the road in front! We could just watch from across the road—hey—we don't even have to buy nothin' if we don't want—jist pass by and stop and take a look—

(SHE comes in front of Sally again, blocking her way, again SALLY pushes her aside.)

HESTER. ...and then we'll come right on back to church! Come on!

SALLY. I don't think so, Hester! I got to go to Sunday School, and I jist *know* I'd be too scairt!

HESTER. (*Now flouncing away from Sally in the other direction.*) Well, then I'm goin' on by myself—and you ain't never gonna git no chance to see no live Jews or nothin' ever again—not with *me* you ain't! An I'm gonna tell Billy what an ole sissy scaredy cat you are! (*SHE is almost off, then coquettishly SHE turns back.*) Oh my!—I did remember one other thing Billy had said—

SALLY. (*Almost off in other direction, but her curiosity is too great. SHE stops, turns.*) What?

HESTER. (*Coming back toward her, giggling.*) The Jew men got theirselves horns on their heads!

(*SHE laughs out loud now and SALLY starts giggling too, imagining this. HESTER now pursues this.*)

HESTER. And know what *else*?
SALLY. (*Still giggling, succumbs.*) What?
HESTER. They wears *hats* all day long and *never* takes 'em off—jist to hide them horns!

(*This sends them BOTH into more fits of laughter.*)

SALLY. No! I never heard such a thing in my life!
HESTER. And know what *else*?
SALLY. What?
HESTER. They got *tails!*

(*SHE laughs more and SALLY does too.*)

SALLY. TAILS??? Oh Lawd! TAILS??
HESTER. Billy says—(*SHE is convulsed.*) Billy—Billy says—they wears long *coats* to cover *them* up—
SALLY. Land a Goshen, Hester! (*SHE is laughing hysterically.*) Land!
HESTER. Hey—come on—come an go! You know you're jist *dyin'* to see it all! You jist *know* you are! Come on!!! (*And SHE takes her hand pulling her in the direction of the edge of town.*)
SALLY. Oh, Hester—Oh, Hester, I shouldn't—I jist shouldn't go at all—(*But SHE is allowing herself to be pulled.*) Well, we can't stay long—we got to git right back fast, hear??? Promise me that!
HESTER. (*As they BOTH exit, running.*) Sure, sure! Now come on—come on—Ooooeeee!!!

(*As LIGHTS fade we hear the GIRLS singing as THEY run along the country road; it is a popular song from long ago.*)

SALLY & HESTER. (*Offstage.*)
"Oh, we belong to Uncle Sam,
Sing-song Kitsy Kitsy Kai-me-oh.
We belong to Uncle Sam,
Sing-song Kitsy Kitsy Kai-me-oh.
Kay-mo, Kai-mo, dear old Dad,
M'hey, M'hi, M'hum-drum
I go way, we go way, they go way
Uruguay, Paraguay,
Oh! We belong to Uncle Sam!
Sing-song Kitsy Kitsy Kai-me-oh!"

(*Their VOICES fade as we come up on another part of the road which runs diagonally. There is a wagon filled with apples on one side of it and some bushes on the other. Hester and Sally's voices die out as THEY come onstage, and spying the apple wagon, stop, hiding themselves behind the bush, warily looking out, whispering.*)

HESTER. There it is—now all we gotta do is wait—here—stay here—and be quiet and wait—

SALLY. (*Rapidly losing her courage.*) Oh, I jist feel so funny Hester! I truly do! I don't know what it's gonna be like seein' no Jews. But it *sure* feels evil! It bein' Sunday and all! It jist feels EVIL—Oh, HESTER—

(*SARAH now enters, carrying a sign, laboriously handmade and handwritten that says: "APPLES 5¢." She is the oldest daughter of the family. She is a teenager also. Wears a babushka on her head and a long dark skirt and black stockings. SHE looks very European, Semitic. SHE now sticks the sign on the wagon and rearranges the fruit a little. THE GIRLS are whispering.*)

SALLY. Oh, Land! Look at her with that ole funny scarf and all—and so dark! She looks evil Hester! Jist so evil!

HESTER. (*Intrigued.*) Hey—know what they say?

SALLY. (*Wishing she hadn't come.*) What?

HESTER. All their women opens up sideways down there—

SALLY. (*Shocked.*) What?

HESTER. Chink women does too—slanty like their eyes! (*SHE giggles.*) Jist like a cat!

SALLY. Stop that! Don't you go talkin' filthy dirty like that on the Lord's day. Oh, Hester don't! We're gonna git punished for sure—lightnin' or thunder or tornadoes or—

HESTER. Oh hush up, scaredy cat! Ain't nothin gonna happen to us—

SALLY. Well don't you talk dirty like that again!

HESTER. (*Giggling.*) Ain't dirty—it's a fact a life!

(*SARAH turns and now exits.*)

HESTER. Hey—know what else is a fact a life?

SALLY. No—and I don't wanna! I jist want outta here!

HESTER. Their men is in two parts down there—

SALLY. Huh?

HESTER. They cut 'em in half down there when they's babies. They got two dinghies!

SALLY. (*Stunned.*) Oh Land and they livin' HERE?!? PLEASE!!! LET'S GO!! (*SHE grabs her hand, tries to pull her away.*)

HESTER. NO! Let go! I wanna see her some more—besides she's jist a girl. She can't hurt us—but you better not bring your brother round here 'cause they kill other people's baby *boys.* Now that's a fact a—

(*SARAH now reappears carrying a stack of baskets for her apples. SHE hears and sees Sally and Hester.*)

SARAH. (*Speaks hesitantly, with a heavy accent. These are memorized phrases SHE doesn't understand.*) Hello—Hello—How—are—you—? (*SHE starts to cross the road, trying to see them behind the tree, shading her eyes. Now SHE points back to*

wagon. These words SHE understands.) Apples? 5¢? —Du vielst?
(*Trans.: Do you want?*)

SALLY. (*Terrified now.*) Oh Law! She's talkin' jibberty jaw!
She's puttin' some kinda curse on us, Hester! Oh Law!

HESTER. (*Now takes a stand against Sarah, stepping out into
the road.*) No! Don't you come no step closer to us! We don't want
nothin' off you! We don't want no stolen apples!

SARAH. (*Not comprehending at all.*) "Stolen?" Ich forshtayin
zee nisht! (*Trans: I don't understand you!*) (*Again SHE points to
her apples.*) Apples? 5¢? (*SHE steps closer.*)

SALLY. Oh Law! She cursed us again! On my Stars! Let's run!
She's a *witch*!

HESTER. (*Refusing to be intimidated.*) No! I said no! We don't
want your stolen apples! And you keep off a us! This here's a
public road and you keep away, you hear. Or I'll git my Pa! You
got no business here! That's stolen goods!

SARAH. (*Smiling, holding out basket.*) Hello—how—are—
you—(*Her smile fades. SHE sees something is very wrong.*) Vos
iss de mer—vos iss de mer mitt ouns? (*Trans: What is the matter—
what is the matter with you?*)

(*At the Yiddish, HESTER, terrified, grabs stone, hurls it, hitting
SARAH on the arm. Her baskets fall to the ground and SARAH
cries out in pain. At this SALLY breaks away and starts running
off, screaming.*)

SALLY. WITCH! WITCH!!

HESTER. Now you keep away from us! Don't you put no curse
on us. JIST KEEP AWAY!! JIST KEEP AWAY!! (*SHE is backing
up, holding Sarah at bay, then runs off.*)

SARAH. (*SHE stands, sobbing, holding her arm. After a beat,
with bitter anger, SHE screams after them.*) SHIKSAS!!!
SHIKSAS!!! (*Trans: Gentile girls! Gentile girls!*) (*After a moment
SHE wipes her eyes, picks up her pile of baskets and goes to the
wagon, stacking them on the ground. Then determinedly, SHE
takes her sign and sticks it in the front row of apples so it will be
more visible. Then SHE turns and looks down the road in the

direction of the girls. After a moment, SHE yanks her babushka from her head and twists it quickly into a long cord. SHE now gathers her long dark hair at the nape of her neck and ties it with the cord in the manner of Sally and Hester. SHE now looks down the road the other way for her next customers; with as much bravado as she can muster, hiding her fear. SHE begins reciting.) "Hello? How are you? Apples, 5¢. Hello? How are you—"

(In the distance, we hear SALLY and HESTER singing as they run along the country road to church.)

SALLY & HESTER. (*Offstage.*)
"Oh, we belong to Uncle Sam,
Sing-song Kitsy Kitsy Kai-me-oh.
We belong to Uncle Sam—"

(Their voices grow fainter and fainter as we go to BLACK.)

THE END

GOING NOWHERE APACE

A play

by Glen Merzer

Going Nowhere Apace premiered at the Actors Theatre of Louisville on June 5, 1989. It was directed by Zan Sawyer-Dailey and had the following cast:

JUDD ....David Burke
FRAN ....Sharyn Jensen
CECILIA ....Marion Zweng
MARY ....Mary Evans Lott

Scenic Designer: Paul Owen
Sound Designer: Mark Hendren
Property Master: Mark Bissonnette
Production Stage Manager: Carey Upton
Costume Designer: Kevin McLeod
Lighting Designer: Jan Thornsberry
Technical Director: Steve Goodin
Production Managers: Bob Krakower, J. Christopher Wineman
Dramaturg: Julie Crutcher

GOING NOWHERE APACE

FRANCESCA, JUDD, CECILIA, and MARY are all riding their exercycles at a good clip. JUDD pedals along between FRANCESCA and CECILIA; MARY is to the other side of Cecilia. There are no other exercycles. The WOMEN stare straight ahead as they exercise; JUDD steals a few glances to either side, as if his mind is on other things than fitness. Finally HE smiles at Francesca.

JUDD. Maintaining eighty?

FRANCESCA. Excuse me?

JUDD. Are you maintaining eighty r.p.m.?

FRANCESCA. Yes.

JUDD. Me too. (*Pause.*) How's your pulse?

FRANCESCA. Fine.

JUDD. Not me. (*Indicating dial on his bike.*) According to this, I'm legally dead. No pulse at all. I'm not just getting in shape, I'm confronting my mortality. (*Pause.*) That's all right by me. People don't think enough about death, anyway. In my opinion. (*Pause.*) You don't mind that I'm talking to you, do you?

FRANCESCA. No.

JUDD. What's your name?

FRANCESCA. Francesca.

JUDD. Pretty name.

FRANCESCA. Thank you.

JUDD. I'm Judd.

FRANCESCA. Hello.

JUDD. Sometimes you start a conversation with a woman, you don't know if she thinks you're a creep just because you're a man.

FRANCESCA. I don't. Think you're a creep just because you're a man.

JUDD. Good. (*Pause.*) I was saying ...

FRANCESCA. You were saying?

193

JUDD. People don't think enough about death.

(A moment.)

FRANCESCA. What makes you say that?

JUDD. Just making conversation. *(Pause.)* Now if people thought more about death, what do you think would happen?

FRANCESCA. They'd get depressed.

JUDD. No. Happier.

FRANCESCA. Why?

JUDD. They'd realize, hey, someday I'm going to die, so while I'm riding my bike here going absolutely nowhere, I might as well smile at the person next to me, say hello, pass the time pleasantly. And then that would cheer a person up. I know some very morbid people—happiest people I ever met. One of them, for example, real bright lady, philosophy professor, with a huge gap between her front teeth, she could french-kiss with her mouth closed, she's totally obsessed by the image of her own burial. Never stops giggling. Another guy, he reads the obituaries every day, gets a big kick out of sending sympathy cards that rhyme to the widows and signing them "Elvis."

FRANCESCA. How do you know all these morbid people?

JUDD. Can't tell you.

FRANCESCA. All right.

(A long moment.)

JUDD. A therapy group. I belong to a therapy group for morbid people. I'm not supposed to talk about it.

FRANCESCA. All right.

(A moment.)

JUDD. Another guy, a bank teller, fat, jolly type, he looks at you, he sees your skeleton. Can't get it out of his head. Looks at a pretty face, sees a skull.

FRANCESCA. That's awful. Are you like that?

JUDD. No. I see a pretty face, I'm attracted.

FRANCESCA. Why do these people go for therapy if they're so happy?

JUDD. Guilt. Guilt is the major drawback to morbid living. No one feels good about death perkin' him up.

FRANCESCA. Is that your problem?

JUDD. No. My problem is ... I shouldn't discuss it.

FRANCESCA. All right.

(A moment.)

JUDD. I think of death during sex. I'll be fondling a breast, I'll imagine worms gnawing away at it.

FRANCESCA. Yeech.

JUDD. Yeah. I'll actually have thoughts like that.

FRANCESCA. And does that—does that make you happy, too?

JUDD. No. But it does keep me from coming too soon. *(Pause.)* Am I being too vulnerable with you?

FRANCESCA. Not at all.

JUDD. I don't confide in people easily. Do you?

FRANCESCA. Yes.

JUDD. I wish I could.

FRANCESCA. I figure otherwise I'd have to go to confession. And I'm a very tactile person. I don't see the point in confiding in someone without touching. Do you belong to any organized religion?

JUDD. No, I'm Jewish. *(Pause.)* Could I maybe take you to dinner sometime?

FRANCESCA. No.

JUDD. How's your speed?

FRANÇESCA. Fine.

JUDD. Pulse?

FRANCESCA. Good.

(A moment.)

JUDD. Why not?

FRANCESCA. I don't know how to answer that question.

(A moment.)

JUDD. Why not?

FRANCESCA. I'm not attracted to you.

JUDD. No, I meant why don't you know how to answer that question.

FRANCESCA. It's hard to do tactfully.

JUDD. Then forget it. Don't even try.

(A long moment. FRANCESCA once again stairs straight ahead as she pedals. JUDD slowly turns to CECILIA, smiles at her.)

JUDD. Hi.

CECILIA. Hi.

JUDD. Are you maintaining eighty r.p.m.?

CECILIA. Ninety-five.

JUDD. Very good. How's your pulse?

CECILIA. Oh, that does not matter to me. I don't look for that really.

JUDD. Where are you from?

CECILIA. Sweden.

JUDD. I thought so. You've got just a little bit of an accent.

CECILIA. Oh, I have very much an accent!

JUDD. No, just a little one. What's your name?

CECILIA. Cecilia.

JUDD. Pretty name. I'm Judd.

CECILIA. Nice to meet you.

JUDD. Nice to meet *you. (Pause.)* I hear people commit suicide a lot in Sweden.

CECILIA. Well, yes, too much.

JUDD. *Too much* is a value judgment; the point is you have a very high rate over there. Why do you think that is? I mean, you have everything in Sweden, don't you? You're all filthy rich, absolutely stunning people, the state looks after your welfare, you have a peaceful society, not even a prayer of racial antagonism, the

Volvo is a terrific make of car, why do you suppose your people go around killing themselves the way they do?

CECILIA. It's not so many people. It's only a ... minority.

JUDD. I should hope so. But it's a silent minority, wouldn't you say? I mean, it's not your noisy, American breed of suicider, who generally uses a shotgun and takes a few innocent bystanders with him sort of as chasers. No, your people just down a few extra pills and go to sleep, and if they leave a note it's undoubtedly short, considerate, and typed on nice letterhead. Am I right?

CECILIA. Some scientists say it's because the nights. We have very long, dark nights in Sweden.

JUDD. Still, you don't have to kill yourself. You could turn a light on.

CECILIA. It has a biologic effect, they say, the long nights. On the brain.

JUDD. Could be.

CECILIA. But nobody really knows why.

JUDD. Have you lost many friends to the dark nights?

CECILIA. No. One person I hardly knew at university—

JUDD. I lost more than that. I lost a girl friend.

CECILIA. I'm sorry.

JUDD. Well, she wasn't technically a girl friend yet. But I was really looking forward to a relationship with her. And I think she was looking forward to a relationship with me. (*Pause.*) Although I suppose she might not have been as gung ho.

CECILIA. I'm sorry, what is *gung ho*?

JUDD. What is *gung ho*? For example, I'm enormously attracted to you, Cecilia. Could I take you to dinner tomorrow night?

CECILIA. No.

JUDD. Okay, you see, *you* are not gung ho. You see?

CECILIA. I'm sorry, I am married.

JUDD. Dammit, Cecilia! Why did you withhold that information? Jesus!

CECILIA. I did not—

JUDD. You're not wearing a ring—

CECILIA. I don't like to—

JUDD. You knew I was interested—

CECILIA. No, I—

JUDD. The proper thing to do—maybe you're not aware of American customs—the proper thing to do, Cecilia, in a situation like this is to mention your husband in conversation. For example, we were chatting about suicide in Sweden, you could have said, my *husband* attributes this phenomenon to our long, dark nights. You could have said that and spared my feelings.

CECILIA. I'm sorry but—

JUDD. Is it mainly the men who kill themselves in Sweden? I'll bet it is. I'll bet it's the men who dive headlong into those long, dark nights. I'll see you around.

(JUDD hops off his bike, and jogs behind Cecilia's bike and Mary's bike. HE runs in place next to MARY, who tries not to notice him. MARY is wearing headphones; a cassette player is strapped to her belt. JUDD mimes removing the headphones as HE runs in place. HE has to perform this mime several times before MARY notices and removes her headphones.)

JUDD. Hi. *(Pause.)* Are you maintaining eighty r.p.m.?

MARY. Yeah. Why?

JUDD. *(As HE jogs in place.)* Me too. How's your pulse?

MARY. Why?

JUDD. Just interested.

MARY. Fuck off.

(A silence. The THREE WOMEN keep pedalling away, facing straight ahead. MARY puts her headphones back on. JUDD jogs in place, then turns and jogs away, then suddenly turns again, jogs back towards Mary, rips her headphones off her ears, and, choking with emotion, explains himself.)

JUDD. Look forgive me I'm a human being, I'm reaching out, please, I'm only asking, I need to talk to someone or I may I may lose my—please, the world beats down on you and down on you and I'm, I'm, help me, I don't know if I can take people's cruelty anymore, all I'm asking is to have a little simple talking interaction token of human kindness! I'm losing my breath.

(HE takes a long, deep breath. MARY is frozen, stunned by this onslaught. JUDD looks at her, feels that he has won his point, and slows down to a walking pace.)

JUDD. Do you mind if I just walk while we talk? *(JUDD smiles, walks in place.)* I'm perfectly harmless, I really am.

(A moment, as JUDD walks in place, and MARY, still stunned, stares at him.)

JUDD. I'm sorry. I'm sorry. *(HE reaches over to put her headphones back over her ears.)* Forget it. Have a good day.

(HE turns to walk away, but just as he does so, MARY removes her headphones.)

MARY. What do you want to talk about?
JUDD. *(Smiles. HE will continue to walk in place throughout his conversation with Mary.)* What's your name?
MARY. Mary. *(A moment.)*
JUDD. Pretty name. Where are you from?
MARY. Cincinnati. *(Pause.)* And you?
JUDD. I'm from Lexington but my ancestors go back to Long Island. On the East Coast. *(Pause.)* Well, tell me something about yourself, Mary.
MARY. What do you want to know? I'm a word processor.
JUDD. High-stress occupation.
MARY. I know.
JUDD. I was reading there are a lot of strokes among word processors. A lot of early deaths. They don't know why. Either the stress or else some kind of radiation they haven't discovered yet emanating from the terminals.

(A moment.)

MARY. What do you do?

(A moment.)

JUDD. I'm currently between transitions. (*Pause.*) What's your most embarrassing memory?
MARY. Why?
JUDD. I'll bet you've got some good ones.
MARY. I can think of one but it's personal.
JUDD. Tell me.
MARY. I don't even know you!
JUDD. My name's Judd.
MARY. What's your problem, Judd? I mean, what got you so upset a minute ago? You sounded desperate.

(A moment.)

JUDD. Oh. Oh, *that*. That was nothing, really. I was just feeling a little low for a moment there. (*Pause.*) All right, all right, I'm denying. (*Pause.*) I'm scared to leave myself open. I don't confide in people easily, do you?
MARY. Yeah, my friends.
JUDD. Well, I wish I could. I wish I could be as open as you. You know what it goes back to? It goes back to, little girls are allowed to cry in our society and little boys aren't. Which is sick. Either *we* should be allowed to cry, too, or else girls shouldn't be. (*Pause.*) The fact is, Mary, I'll be honest … I haven't been happy lately. I've been unhappy, in fact.
MARY. Why?
JUDD. Let me ask you this, Mary: Where did you meet your current boyfriend or husband?
MARY. I don't have a current boyfriend or husband.
JUDD. Okay, most people meet them at work. Studies have verified that the work environment facilitates flirtation and courtship far better than other environments such as leisure environments in which people are generally preoccupied.

Consequently I find myself at a strategic disadvantage.

MARY. I don't follow you.

JUDD. It's a chicken-and-egg problem. Can I get motivated to work or will I just get more mystified by the aloneness that develops from interpersonal confusion?

(A moment.)

MARY. What does that have to do with a chicken and egg?

JUDD. I'm not presently employed. I can't seem to choose an area of ... I can't concentrate long enough to ... I'm on S.S.I. I had to fill out a form. *Tell in your own words* why you can't earn your living. *(Pause.)* I made up my own words. *(Pause.)* I used to work, moving shit back and forth, but working made me think of death which was the last thing I needed to think about given the type of worker I was.

MARY. What type of worker were you?

JUDD. Slow. I was too slow. *(Pause.)* The problem is, I don't work, so I only get to meet people when they're out in the world and being unfriendly ... because people don't talk to people who they can't be sure who they are, whether they're stable, solid citizens, see—they're scared of them, so what happens is ... what happens is ... I can't break through ... it's a vicious cycle ... I never get *taken in* by anybody, you know? I'm like a dog that's always out on the stoop. I never get *taken in*.

(A long moment.)

MARY. My roommate walked in on me once while I was having sex.

JUDD. WHAT?

MARY. My roommate walked in on me once while I was having sex. You wanted to know my most embarrassing moment. That was it.

JUDD. You just tell me a thing like that out of the blue? Your roommate—why are you telling me this? Christ Almighty, Mary, are you trying to make me jealous?

MARY. No, I'm—

JUDD. I never realized you had this uninhibited side to you!

MARY. I was just—

JUDD. What a story! Your roommate walks in and—bam! That's unbelievable! That's a fucking unbelievable story! (*Pause.*) Could I maybe have your phone number and take you out sometime?

MARY. No. No, I don't think that would be a good idea.

JUDD. What was your roommate's reaction? What did your roommate say?

MARY. She said excuse me.

JUDD. Unbelievable! She really said *excuse me*? And what did you do?

(*A moment.*)

MARY. I was busy.

JUDD. You didn't stop?

MARY. Well … she excused herself and left right away.

JUDD. Did you laugh? Did you and the guy laugh about it?

MARY. No.

JUDD. Really? You really didn't laugh? You just kept going?

MARY. Yes.

JUDD. Like nothing happened?

MARY. I got rid of my roommate, though. For being so inconsiderate.

JUDD. That's amazing. Did you ever discuss the incident with your roommate?

MARY. Not in so many words.

JUDD. But you evicted her?

MARY. Yes.

JUDD. Am I the first person you told about it?

(*A moment.*)

MARY. Yes.

JUDD. Well, I'm just bowled over. I am bowled over by the

trust you've placed in me! I don't know what I've done to earn it. (*Pause.*) Why did you choose me? Why did you choose me as the first person you'd confide in? (*Pause.*) Well, let me tell you, Mary, I will think of that story every time I see a word processor. I will think of that story, and I will remember how oblivious people can be, and it'll put a smile on my face! (*Pause.*) You really kept going just like nothing happened?

(*MARY is not even looking at him anymore; her face is set in a determined mask and SHE is pedalling furiously.*)

JUDD. (*Smiles.*) You really did, didn't you?

(*Chuckling to himself, JUDD jogs away and exits. The THREE WOMEN, looking straight ahead, keep pedalling away. Very slowly the LIGHTS fade to BLACK.*)

THE END

PROCEDURE

by Joyce Carol Oates

Procedure premiered at the Actors Theatre of Louisville on December 16, 1991. It was directed ty William McNulty. The cast was:

A. ....Leslie Beatty
B. ....Stacey Leigh Ivey

Scenic Design: Paul Owen
Costume Designer: Kevin McLeod
Lighting Designer: Casey Clark
Sound Designer: Darron West
Production Manager: Bob Krakower
Stage Manager: Lauren McDonald
Dramaturg: Amy Smith
Property Master: Mark Bissonnette

CHARACTERS

A.—late twenties or early thirties
B.—younger and less assured

TIME & PLACE

The present.
A hospital room, and a nurses' lounge

PROCEDURE

LIGHTS up. In a hospital bed, motionless, lies the BODY of a man. He is not elderly; perhaps in his sixties. An IV tube is attached to one of his nostrils; another tube snakes beneath the bedclothes, in the region of his groin. There may be a white screen partly enclosing the bed. A bedside table, with a minimum of items on it. From stage right enter two nurses' aides—A. and B. A. is in her late twenties or early thirties; brisk, self-assured, practiced in her movements. B. is not only younger but less assured; her movements are occasionally faltering and timid, but not excessively. B. is in every sense the apprentice, determined to learn PROCEDURE, and eager to acquit herself well. Both A. and B. are healthy, even husky young women, and both exhibit near-faultless posture. Between them THEY are carrying the "Death Pack" equipment—a kit out of which items (see below) will be taken, plus a small laundry hamper, a large paper bag, two white sheets, a stretcher and litter straps.

The predominate color of the set is white: stark, dazzling white. The nurses' uniforms, stockings, shoes; the dead patient's gown; the bedclothes. A penumbra of darkness surrounds.

A. and B. approach the bed, B. just perceptibly hesitant.

A. (*Sharp, clear, mechanical voice.*) PROCEDURE. Open the Death Pack. (*B. opens the Death Pack.*) Take out the DO NOT ENTER sign. (*B. does so.*) Affix to outside of patient's door.

(*B. takes out the sign, which measures about 12" by 8", "DO NOT ENTER" in bold black letters; hangs from the outside doorknob of a door at the rear.*)

B. (*Nervous smile, breathless laugh.*) I guess—anybody out in the hall, they'd sure know what we were doing.

A. (*Freezing B. out by continuing, in the same voice.*)
PROCEDURE. Remove the contents of the Death Pack and set on
available surface in patient unit.

(*B. follows A's instructions, fumbling now and then; conspicuously
not looking at the dead man.*)

A. One wrapping sheet. Absorbent cotton. Padding. Bandage
rolls. Safety pins. Death tags.
B. (*Softly, as if dead man might overhear.*) This is—my first
time. My first—(*Gestures awkwardly, abashedly.*)

(*A. gives B. a look of reproof. A beat.*)

A. PROCEDURE. Remove treatment equipment, if any, from
patient unit.

(*B. detaches IV tube, etc., with A.'s assistance; pushes equipment
to the side.*)

A. Lower the head rest, leaving a single pillow.

(*B. lowers head rest, fumbling a bit. Forgets to remove a pillow.*)

A. LEAVING A SINGLE PILLOW.
B. (*Quickly.*) Oh yes—sorry!

(*B. places one pillow on the floor; the dead man's head lolls,
which alarms her. As A. gestures impatiently, B. adjusts the
head. Her facial expression is taut, but does not betray
distaste.*)

B. Poor guy—wonder who he was!
A. (*Continuing, perhaps more forcibly; in an incantatory,
ritual-like manner.*) PROCEDURE. Place the body of the deceased
in as natural a position as possible—arms at sides (*A. and B. do
this, B. a bit timidly.*); palms turned toward thighs. (*B. does this.*)

B. (*Breathlessly.*) Wonder *why*—"palms toward thighs."

A. (*Coolly.*) PROCEDURE. (*A beat.*) Close eyelids gently.

B. (*Nervous laugh.*) Gee—whyn't they have us do this *first*?—so, y'know, the—, the—, *he* isn't looking at us, like! (*Tries to close eyelids, without success.*) Oh my God—they won't *close*.

A. (*As before.*) Close eyelids gently.

B. (*Tries again.*) Oh mister, I wish you'd c-cooperate, I'm just kind of, kind of—NERVOUS. (*SHE succeeds in shutting both eyelids.*) Hey—O.K.! Thank God.

(*B. holds out her hands, for A. to see how they are shaking. But A. is indifferent.*)

A. PROCEDURE. If the deceased has dentures—

B. (*Pointing, frightened; as one eyelid opens slowly.*) Oh—he's waking up!

(*A., though exasperated with B., says nothing. In a quick, fluid, decisive manner SHE draws her fingertips down over both the dead man's eyelids; this time both eyelids remain shut.*)

B. Oh!—how'd you do that? (*Pause; abashed.*) Well—I guess I'll learn.

A. If the deceased has dentures, these should be cleaned and—

B. (*Nervous attempt at humor.*) They *all* have dentures, seems like!

A. (*Continuing, without inflection.*)—cleaned and replaced in mouth.

B. (*Misunderstanding, leans over to peer at dead man's mouth preparatory to timidly poking her fingers into it.*) Oh—mister! You're gonna have to ex-cuse me—

A. (*Irritated, but maintaining decorum.*) Dentures should be cleaned and REPLACED. (*As if in an aside, now that she is not repeating instructions from the handbook.*) You must know—dentures are not *in* the patient's mouth. (*Points to bedside table.*)

B. Oh! Sorry! (*B. locates dentures in a glass on the table. Picks them up hesitantly. Holds to light.*) They look O.K. to me. I mean—clean. (*Peering; with a shivery laugh.*) Must be weird, wearing 'em. False teeth!

A. (*Coolly, as if making a pronouncement.*) Nothing is "weird" in this place.

B. (*Approaching patient.*) Well, excuse me, mister, gotta put these back *in*. So that your folks, coming to see you in the—the—downstairs—

A. In the morgue.

B. —so they'll see you at your best.

(*B. mimes replacing dentures in mouth. [Specific action may be hidden, or disguised, by portable bed screen.] Has difficulties, murmuring to herself.*)

B. Oh—damn—I just don't know *how*. Like, in real life, this guy'd do it *himself*. (*To A., pleading.*) Y'know—he's still warm. His mouth, I mean. Inside. Wet too—saliva. (*A pause. B. backs away, suddenly frightened.*) Oh God—that's a dead man!

A. (*In official voice.*) Sometimes, with the dead, dentures cannot be replaced. (*Looking on as B. tries gamely again.*) DO NOT FORCE.

(*B. fumbles dentures, drops to floor.*)

B. (*Aghast.*) Oh God! I'm sorry!

A. (*Picking up dentures, setting on table, continuing as before.*) PROCEDURE. Replace top bedding with draping sheet.

(*B. covers body awkwardly with large sheet, removes other sheet. The next several steps are done under the sheet, with some difficulty, and distaste, by B.*)

A. Remove patient's pajamas. (*B. does so, folding and thrusting them into a laundry hamper as quickly as possible.*) Press bladder gently to expel accumulated urine. (*B. does so.*) Remove catheter. (*B. does so.*) Place cotton pads over rectum and genitalia to absorb feces and urine which will be expelled as sphincters relax.

B. (*As she is doing this.*) Oh!—oh dear. I guess we had a little accident.

(*A. tosses B. a towel or more absorbent cotton. B. wipes, under the sheet.*)

B. (*Trying not to appear repelled.*) It's just so—oh geez what can you *say.* You start out life soiling your diapers and you end—

A. Clean old adhesive markings from skin, if any.

B. (*Peering under sheet.*) Poor guy—he's got 'em. (*B. busies herself with this task.*)

A. Prop sagging jaw with folded pads.

B. That's how *my* mouth comes open, if I sleep on my back! I hear this wet-sort-of noise, y'know, in my sleep, it wakes me up sometimes, or, a minute later, I'm *snoring—*(*As SHE props up dead man's jaw, with some initial difficulty.*) I'm gonna be so worried someday, when—if—

A. Pad ankles with cotton and tie together with bandage.

B. (*As SHE does this.*)—I'm married, or something. (*Pause.*) My father, he snores so you can hear it through the whole—

A. (*Making out tags, deftly.*) PROCEDURE. Tie one signed tag to right great toe (*Gives B. the tag.*)—tie one signed tag to left wrist.

B. Why *two*? The toe and the wrist aren't gonna get separated, are they?

A. Roll body gently to side of bed. (*A. helps B. do this.*) Place one clean sheet diagonally under body. (*Pause.*) DIAGONALLY under body. (*Pause.*) Roll body back to center of sheet.

B. (*Shivering.*) He's still warm—some places. Just his fingers and toes, and his face, are *real* cold. (*Pause.*) Looks like kind of a nice guy, don't he?—'course any man, no matter how cruel, he's gonna look nice, peaceful, sort of, in a weird way, like a *woman*, at a time like this. Y'know what I mean—?

A. (*Freezing B. out.*) Fold upper corner of sheet loosely over the head and face—(*As THEY do so.*)—the lower corner over the feet (*Etc.*)

B. (*Almost giddy with strain, waving to patient.*) Bye-bye!

A. Secure the arms at the sides by bringing the right and left corners of the sheet over to complete the wrapping.

B. (*Performs this action swiftly, keeping pace with A.'s words.*) Yeah! Right!

A. Fasten sheet with safety pins. (*Tosses pins to B.*) Fasten additional signed tag to outside of sheet. (*Etc.*) If dentures could not be replaced, wrap in gauze, identify, pin dentures next to tag. (*Etc.*)

B. He could be anybody now ...

A. Lift wrapped body to stretcher.

B. Here's the hard part, huh? (*A. and B. lift body, lay on stretcher, which is on the floor; THEY have less difficulty than might be expected.*)—Geeze he's *light* isn't he!

A. Fasten litter straps at chest—(*THEY do so.*)—and just above the knees. (*Etc.*) Cover body with additional sheet.

B. (*Immense sigh.*) Well—that's that.

A. (*Continuing as before, with perhaps the slightest suggestion of sharing B.'s relief.*) PROCEDURE. Transfer body quietly and with dignity to the morgue, avoiding if possible public entrances and lobbies—

B. (*As A. and B. pick up ends of the stretcher, in a loud, somewhat giddy voice.*)—"QUIETLY and with DIGNITY to the morgue—avoiding PUBLIC ENTRANCES AND LOBBIES." Yeah! You bet!

(*LIGHTS down as A. and B. exit with stretcher.*
LIGHTS up. A. and B. are alone, apparently in a nurses' lounge; both have cans of soda which THEY open, and drink from; A. lights a cigarette, and offers one to B.)

B. (*Still shaky.*) I—uh, thanks but I—I'm not smoking now. I mean, I'm trying not to. (*Wipes face with tissue.*) Well. Sure glad I don't work in the *morgue*.

A. (*Imperturbably.*) It's quiet in the morgue.

B. I'll say!

A. (*Regarding her quizzically; almost friendly.*) It wasn't so bad, was it?

B. (*Laughing.*) To tell the truth, yes.

A. Just following procedure.

B. Procedure—! (*Shudders.*)

A. Not the first time you saw a dead patient, was it?

B. No, not exactly. But the first time I ... touched one.

A. (*Clinical interest.*) And how was it?

B. (*Staring at A., perplexed.*) How was it? (*Pause.*) It was—something I won't forget.

A. You won't?

B. I sure *won't.*

(*A beat or two. A. regards B. as if bemused. BOTH sip from cans.*)

A. (*Casually.*) That man—dead man I mean—he was my father. (*Picking tobacco off tongue, as B. stares at her.*) I mean—that man, when living, had been my father.

B. (*Staring, blinking.*)—What?

A. Him. Just now. My father.

B. You're—joking!

A. Why would I joke? (*Half-smile.*) It isn't my practice to joke.

B. But—I don't believe it. Him—(*Points vaguely offstage.*)—us—*you*—

A. (*Matter-of-factly.*) I should explain—I hadn't seen him in a while. We weren't close.

B. Oh! You weren't "close."

A. He left us when I was sixteen. Didn't remarry or anything, just left. He lived in the city—I'd run into him sometimes—we'd talk, sort of. Sometimes, he'd avoid me. (*Pause.*) Or I'd avoid him.

B. Did you know he was here in the hospital?

A. Sure.

B. Did you know he was—dying?

A. More or less.

B. And you didn't tell anyone?

A. (*As if genuinely baffled.*) Didn't tell anyone—?

B. Oh—any of the nurses, or—

A. Why should I?—I'm a professional. I do my job.

B. And it didn't upset you to, to—

A. I said, I'm a professional. He wasn't *my* first.
B. (*Slight attack of dizziness.*) Oh—!

(*A. helps B., as B. leans forward, touching forehead to knees.*)

A. You're all right.
B. (*Recovering.*) I'm—all right. (*Pause.*) C'n I have a—?

(*A. passes the package of cigarettes to B., who takes one, lights it, exhales smoke gratefully.*)

B. (*Emphatically.*) My God, I'm so—embarrassed. Here I was thinking of myself, mainly. My first—death. (*Pause.*) I wish I could go through it again, now. See how you did it. Knowing what you told me. . .
A. (*Moving off.*) Sorry! It's a scene that can't quite be repeated.

(*LIGHTS out.*)

THE END

THE GOBLINS PLOT TO MURDER GOD

by Mark O'Donnell

CHARACTERS

TELLER

OOZE

BOGLES (Goblins)

THE GOBLINS PLOT TO
MURDER GOD

*This scene is played in wild NEAR-DARKNESS, with glints and
flashes of LIGHT, and only the TELLER's and OOZE's faces
well-lit. The BOGLES are like a ragtag band of medieval
soldiers. The LIGHT comes up to reveal the outline of
mustering little forms in tattered rags and outlandish hoods,
cowls, and helmets. Perhaps the goblins wear pointed noses or
off-putting masks. A clumsy, irregular DRUM and an obscene
primitive FLUTE sound the call to assembly. The TELLER, a
disfigured but at least human figure in awful dark-ages refugee
clothing, eyes the audience and addresses them: He is their
storyteller/narrator. A stylized depiction of God's two great
EYES may surmount the scene.*

TELLER.
Bleak and squeaking, weakly seeking,
To the clumsy drum they come.
Hobbling, wriggling, straggling gaggle—
Niggling goblins! Here are some!
Gabbling rabble, thrum and thrum!
This, their cheerless leader Ooze.
Let us hide and bide what brews.

*(The TELLER steps to the side; OOZE; the most dynamic of the
goblins, asserts himself.)*

OOZE.
Caw! Caw! Caw!
I caw for order.
Are we met?
Gather, slathering hordes, ye wet

and soapless creatures! Gobble-ins!
Here! Your flaps and weepers this way steer!
Behold and hear what hatches now!
Fear makes us know, pain makes us vow!
We all know What, but not yet How!
    BOGLES. Hail,Ooze! Hail, Ooze most Wordy Ruler!

(Long significant pause. Finally:)

    ONE BOGLE. I want something to eat.

(OOZE stares him down harshly.)

    OOZE.
Come, minions of slime, pinioned by time!
Now we begin! In this daily fire
we heat toward Holy War! Let ire
get higher and higher! Mad choir, come—
Bask us in strategies, sprout steel, sharpen your shoes!
Raise spears and spring!
    BOGLES. Sssssssspring! I'faith! I'faith!
    OOZE.
We plan to plant the Prince of Planets—
to surly hurl the world and what began it!
We grease the ground with God! Or will!
    BOGLES. Will! Will!

(Pause.)

    OOZE. Well?

(Awkward silence. There's no actual plan.)

    TELLER. (*To audience.*)
To make it plain, these ogling bogles, acorn-bodied,
acorn-brained,
have ordained a Holy murder.

They crave to crimp Him the O Big One!
Can they do it? Why hate *Him*?
What makes them take His glory grim,
These addled anti-cherubim?
Are they mad? Do flying fish swim?
Your flaps and weepers this way steer—
with weepers, watch—with flaps, now hear!

(Turns attentively to Ooze.)

    OOZE. We chew on theocide!
    BOGLES. We chew!
    OOZE. We plot to put Ubiquity aside!
    BOGLES. We do!
    OOZE.
As you are all despaired, God bodes us bad!
To throw us in the mud and sad—
One breath from death to death is had
and nothing more! Bad God!
    TELLER. (*Aghast.*) Good Gad!
    OOZE.
He makes night fright, He makes day gray,
He gives to take our hopes away!
Robed in welkin, King of Things!
The galaxies his pinkie rings!
His wigglers trees, his tossers, mountains!
His giz is fizz beyond all fountains!
And His ideas, mosquitoes all—
mere whims of Him make empires fall!
If He says dance, then we must crawl!
To budge that badge that holds us thrall,
Now think! Now think!
    TELLER. These plans apall!
    ONE BOGLE. To murder God? It can't be done!
    OOZE.
To bell the cat!
To shoot the Sun!

To take away the All that's one!
Now think! Now think!

    ONE BOGLE. But—

    OOZE. (*Cuffs him violently.*)

Craven shrinker! You haven't even tried your thinker!
One inch of plan brings on the brink!
Does God scare us?

    BOGLES. (*A sort of pep rally.*) No!

    ONE BOGLE. Unless—

    BOGLES. No!

    ANOTHER BOGLE. Although—

    OOZE. (*Impatiently.*) Be certain!

    ANOTHER BOGLE. Yes!

    OOZE. (*Ejecting the coward bogle.*) Once more now—Does God scare us?

    BOGLES. No!!

    OOZE. Will we allow Him to despair us?

    BOGLES. No!

    ONE BOGLE. But God knows that this No's not so.

    OOZE. (*Striking this doubter.*)

If you are frightened, do not say it.
Courage comes when cowards play it!
What's the plan, then? Bogles, bray it!

    ONE BOGLE.

What monster's large enough to devour Him?
So towering to overpower Him?
The greatest beast's to Him an elf!

    ANOTHER BOGLE. Could he be tricked ... into killing Himself?

    TELLER. (*Relieved.*)

Their hopes are mad, but luckily,
their brains as one would fail to fell a flea!

    OOZE.

Your cheerless leader you annointed me,
but Bogles, you have disappointed me.

    ONE BOGLE. It can't be done!

    OOZE. Throw that one out!

(Another BOGLE is ejected from the circle. It's getting small now.)

OOZE.
This bout cannot be won with doubt!
Now percolate! Now spill! Now spout!
Derail for me your train of thought!
Detail your legendary plot!
My ever littler swarm, be rife!
Deform a plan! Give death new life!
TELLER.
This all reminds me of the fable—
the cat-worn mice who were unable
to subdue their feline Lord,
but that they should, were in accord.
OOZE.
Plunk His sleeping weepers from Him!
Plunk his grape-wet globies! Yes!
That's it!
ONE BOGLE. It is? ... I do not follow!
OOZE.
Imagine it! His hallowed hollow
sockets scraped of their Divine—
and in our pockets they might shine
as sweet as stolen coins to urchins.
And He, ha ha, could do no searching—
His this-way-outs we'll have abstracted!
TELLER. Easier plotted than enacted!
OOZE. (*Excited.*)
Fell the highest tree in all Creation!
Fashion then a sharpened pike. And patient
heat it in the hottest coals
until it throbs like hell's own souls,
and in summation, all we have to do—
is find God's eyes, and plunge our pike thereto!
ANOTHER BOGLE.
But—but—the sky's His eyes! Why, the horiz-

on is his brow! The sun and moon's his eyes!
His eyeshine swims through walls and bone!
It burns in us, we turn to stone—
We'll never find His eyes alone!
We welter shelterless and visible!
    TELLER. Sneak up on God? The notion's risible.
    ANOTHER BOGLE.
He mices us, He does! Mere unwinding crumblemush
underfoot and mumblecrush, and in a rush,
underearthly humbleflush. This is Thus
and Thus Is All, The only way to go is fall,
We can't change that at all at all.
    OOZE.
No! Mice will not be mice! Thrash, trash! Lather, cadavers!
Devise, surprise, and alter Never!
    BOGLES. Whirrrrr, whirrrrr, whirrrrr, Words.
    TELLER.
And what are words?
Ever airborne useless birds!
    OOZE. He'll perish by His own parishioners!
    BOGLES. Whirrrr, whirrrrr, whirrrrr, Words.
    OOZE.
We'll throw him down his own throat!
Trickling glitter, under rubble,
cut and luggaged, thugged with trouble,
watering rivulets into the worm-ways,
weeping for his out-of-sights!
New to grue, to grief, to nights!
And meanwhile, Bogles, We, the rising shiners!
Lords and ladylights in angels' fineries
and halos! In our clean snowflaming wrappers,
the stars become us, we become them,
summon harps of joy and strum them,
far above this boggled furnace.
Bogles, burn what wants to burn us!

(The few remaining BOGLES are not convinced, and abandon

Ooze one by one, as if losing interest in a mad street zealot.)

OOZE.
And, I, Ooze, washed white in blood,
King of Aftermath, and you, my Boglephim!
My thrones and dominations, my thorns and diminutions,
my satellites, my ...

(HE persists, but hopelessly, with his fantasy of Heaven.)

The Tatterscript of Word, the Word that, once heard,
obliterates belief in the Absurd,
the Word that will explain the World,
that made the sun voom forth, and sneezed the stars,
I, Ooze, usurper of eternity, trace out its characters
its radiant cuneiform, in the room above the spillyshiny
sweep of the seven heavens, above the all-inclusive treasure,
His glinting store! There, in His windowed skyatop,
His nook, my nook. His book, my book!...

*(There is a clap of LIGHTNING and THUNDER. The BOGLES
scatter. OOZE looks fearfully to the sky, as if retribution is to
strike.)*

OOZE.
They forsook me! You forsake me!
Go on, strike me! Hook me! Bake me!
Incinerate me, please, how freeing!
I am sick to death of being!

*(But instead of immolation, a light shower of ROSES falls gently
about Ooze. HE is dismayed. The BOGLES creep back onstage
curiously as the scene concludes.)*

TELLER.
An unexpected weather from above!
Instead of brimstone, this wronged God drops love!

OOZE. (*Collapsing.*)
You mock me, Maker! Faker of Sublimity!
The Inaccessible feigns Proximity!
Damn You! May You Damn Yourself!
    TELLER. He tries to stab the wind, and so he falls.
    OOZE.
I hear a riddle when the owl calls.
I stare illiterate at Nature's sprawls.
Wax in the rebus, someone, free me!
I cannot see the things that see me!
Amoebus rebus! Rebus, free me!
    TELLER. To fall is all, is all.
    OOZE. O Free me!

*(HE recoils, stung by a thorn on one of the roses.
BLACKOUT.)*

THE END

THE VISIT

by
Lyudmila Petrushevskaya

Translated by Steven Jones

CHARACTERS

MOTHER

SON

DUMMY (a stationary wooden dummy with human form, wearing an institutional cap)

PLACE

A visiting room in a Soviet prison.

THE VISIT

SON finishes what he's eating and wipes his mouth.

MOTHER. Aleksandr Aleksandrovich says hello.

SON. How did he say it?

MOTHER. Tell your son hello, and take heart!

SON. Did you run into him?

MOTHER. Well, I just ... well I called him.

SON. What did he say?

MOTHER. He advised me to get help.

SON. (*Shaking his head.*) Well we didn't need him to tell us that.

MOTHER. He said that he always knew that you weren't like everyone else, and that something would happen to you some day.

SON. Now what are you calling everyone for? Why?

MOTHER. Will you have some fruit compote?

SON. I couldn't get it down.

MOTHER. I'm getting advice, what else can I do? What other choice is there?

SON. I just don't know about you.

MOTHER. I can't sleep at night ... why did you do it?

SON. Shut up! The bastards.

MOTHER. (*Steps back, nods toward the Dummy.*). Will you have some compote? I made it last night. Heavens, so I'd at least have something to do with myself. Last night I called an ambulance, and they gave me something ... They suggested I go to the hospital.

SON. You should have gone.

MOTHER. Sure, and what about you?

SON. For heaven's sake, why are you always making over me? Think about yourself. Who called?

MOTHER. That Boris of yours. He said to say hello.

SON. Who else?

227

MOTHER. Everyone's already done calling, now they're waiting. They're embarrassed, I'm sure.

SON. What do you mean, embarrassed?

MOTHER. Well, it's just ... they feel they're bothering me. And I keep saying the same thing, over and over. Now we're just waiting.

SON. (*Grinning.*) So long! That's it for now. Don't you folks wait.

MOTHER. They allowed me a visit.

SON. Now there, you see? And here's your visit.

MOTHER. On the contrary. I sought advice, and was told I wouldn't get one.

SON. Yes? Why not? Who said that?

MOTHER. The lawyer.

SON. What lawyer? Matveyka?

MOTHER. Someone else.

SON. Did you borrow money again?

MOTHER. It's not a real lawyer, just a legal consultant. A woman. Barskaya is her name.

SON. What did she say?

MOTHER. She said to all appearances, if they gave you a visit, you can expect a good outcome. She had one case where a visit was permitted, and then a pardon was granted. Now they're just waiting for the release. It was fifteen years ago.

SON. What was the crime?

MOTHER. Well ... an especially dangerous crime. Article 508.

SON. There is no such article.

MOTHER. There was, that Barskaya's been around a long time, she's retired now, she works as a consultant, giving consultations. Maybe I got it mixed up.

SON. Well what was it?

MOTHER. Breaking and entering, an old woman and her pregnant niece were murdered. And now he's getting out.

SON. There, you see. There were two of them.

MOTHER. Three. The unborn boy was killed too.

SON. Well now. (*Pause.*) Did anybody else call?

MOTHER. Valeriya didn't call. Yes, Valeriya. Now she's

ended up with a good apartment all to herself, see who you got mixed up with? Like always. She's doing just fine, and you're here. The wrong crowd, it's called.

SON. Momma!

MOTHER. You say Momma, but I warned you that you were biting off more than you could chew. I told you you'd ruin yourself, didn't I? Did I tell you or not? I warned you, and what happened? I was right, that's what. Valeriya's a bitch.

(SON, silent, motions towards the Dummy.)

MOTHER. Well drink some compote. Borisovna brought over some Yugoslavian plums. I am on sick leave, after all. I could be on sick leave for a year, my heart just won't take it. Maslyennikova will extend my leave in a second. "I feel bad dragging you in here to the clinic for an appointment, I'd be happy to write it out to the end right now," she says, "the last thing you need is to be fooling around in here."

SON. To the end of what?

MOTHER. To the end of my life. I won't live through it. And all because of Valeriya. Why with my own bare hands I'd ...

SON. Momma, why did you come here?

MOTHER. Drink your compote. It'll help your digestion. It's good for you.

SON. Do you know how she is?

MOTHER. She's alive, what else.

SON. Does she live alone?

MOTHER. Yes, she's alone. So you can be happy—no one's had any need of her.

SON. Is she working?

MOTHER. No, where would she work?

SON. What do you mean, where would she work?

MOTHER. What are you looking at me like that for, son? Huh? Why I'd like to take that Valeriya and ... Drink your compote, I don't want to carry heavy things back with me.

SON. Tell me, I'll kill you, so help me!

(MOTHER motions with her eyes to the Dummy.)

SON. Please, how is she?
MOTHER. I didn't want to get you upset. Your Valeriya, she's
a bitch, just a bitch. *(Cries.)*
SON. OK, OK, what is it?
MOTHER. She's had the baby, that's what.

(SON stares off into space.)

MOTHER. Your virtuous Valeriya.
SON. A boy or a girl?
MOTHER. A boy, a boy. So as not to forget the father.

(SON throws himself to his knees.)

MOTHER. What are you doing? What are you doing? *(Points
to the Dummy.)*

(SON stands up, then sits.)

MOTHER. Drink your compote.

(SON drinks from the jar.)

MOTHER. Don't forget the berries. She carried him up till the
wedding. Nine months hadn't passed, it was seven and a half. And
showing.
SON. What did they name him?
MOTHER. I didn't ask.
SON. Who'd you talk to?
MOTHER. I called the maternity ward. A boy. Seven pounds,
eight ounces. Twenty inches tall.
SON. How could it be that ...
MOTHER. Well, it's what you want.
SON. Who's going to pick her up now? From the hospital?
MOTHER. Well her girl friends.

SON. No, now she doesn't have anyone to pick her up.

MOTHER. Oh, yes, that's right.

SON. Her mother won't pick her up, neither will her father. Her husband won't ... Their whole family and friends, they're all dead.

MOTHER. That's right.

SON. The neighbors?

MOTHER. What neighbors do you mean? They hadn't even lived there. They got the new apartment all right, but way the hell out in Chertanovka.

SON. Yes ... and she didn't answer a single one of my letters.

MOTHER. She wasn't even at home, she was always off in hospitals ... Took an ambulance right after the wedding.

SON. I remember.

MOTHER. She locked herself in the bathroom.

SON. What was the point of locking herself in, as though I couldn't have broken in ... If I had wanted to. She locked herself in, and that was that; she just didn't want to, and that was all there was to it. I cried and everything. Who called the police?

MOTHER. The downstairs neighbors.

SON. I wouldn't have laid a finger on her. I just wanted to talk with her, just talk. I just wanted those people ... not anybody else. They were the ones that insisted on an abortion, they took her away from me, and then off to the new apartment with no forwarding address! The bastards!

(MOTHER motions toward the Dummy.)

SON. And those girl friends of hers. I came in and they started to laugh. Her mother and father made faces. Her fiance shrugged.

MOTHER. You bit off more than you could chew.

SON. All people are equal! That's what it says. She's my wife.

MOTHER. What are you saying?

SON. She's my wife, damn it! Yes! And he's my son!

MOTHER. (*Uses her eyes and motion to indicate that the Dummy is right next to them.*) For heaven's sake, you.

SON. You can pick her up at the hospital.

MOTHER. You sure do have an imagination.

SON. Buy her ... everything she needs. And send me a note through Matveyka saying who he looks like.

MOTHER. You do have an imagination.

SON. I won't be around for a long time, help her.

MOTHER. We'd have to tell Matveyka that it's your son. How can we do that?

SON. Well what, do you think that would change anything?

MOTHER. She'd deny it. She'd say it wasn't yours.

SON. No, no, they've poisoned her thoughts, she loved me. They talked her ears off and then dug up that jerk somewhere. They did it. She just wasn't feeling well, and they were forcing her to have an abortion.

MOTHER. People don't kill over that.

SON. Oh yeah? The bastards! They wanted to kill my son! They were the ones who wanted to do the killing. What do you think abortion is, anyway?

MOTHER. I know, I know.

SON. And that's why I killed them.

MOTHER. I know, I know.

SON. Her girl friends set everything up for her at the hospital. That Mila and Tomka. Those creeps.

MOTHER. I know.

SON. Mila and Tomka are creeps.

MOTHER. Of course.

SON. Those nurses, them and their abortions ... They're prostitutes. Murderers. Mila and Tomka. They're murderers, giving everyone abortions.

MOTHER. Yes ... That's right ...

SON. They do thirty abortions a day. And I only killed five! You can't even compare it! You can't!

MOTHER. Fine, OK. Just calm down. If that's the way it was, they'll let you out soon. I'll just drop by to see Matveyka and have a few words with her.

SON. (Upset.) Thirty abortions in just one department! And how many hospitals like that one! We're talking about living people! They can hear everything, they eat! They move around! I read about it! Each one has a mother and a father, grandmothers and grandfathers! What, and they have to be killed? Why? They're living children! People have to understand that!

MOTHER. Fine, fine, I know. (*Gathers up jars, leftovers, bags.*)

SON. It's Mila and Tomka, they're the ones who did the killing! It's Valeriya's mother and father and her husband that forced her. There is a God, after all! (*Cries.*) My God, they torture and kill, every day ... Every day, you can't stop it . Take them all to court? You couldn't do it . God have mercy on murdered children ...

MOTHER. We need a doctor right away, right away! You're head doesn't hurt, does it? (*Holding son to her breast.*) Thank God, thank God, I've waited so long! I knew. (*To the Dummy.*) He needs to see a psychiatrist, he's lost his mind, he's a sick man who needs to see a specialist, not be punished. Isolation, not punishment. He's sick, thank God, he's not responsible for his actions ... His thoughts have done this to him ... Who thought up shooting sick people? He killed, and now they'll kill him, but he didn't kill! No! It just seemed that way to him. Let's go home. We'll go home and I'll put you to bed and tuck you in ... You're bunk is waiting for you. Everything's all clean, I swept up, when I felt better. I didn't clean for a long time, but then yesterday I felt better and picked up. Borisovna brought plums from Yugoslavia ... You'll get better ... Your head hurts ... Let's go, I'll take you home ... Quiet now ... (*Looks at the Dummy.*) I can't take him? He's ill. He's lost his mind. (*Looks at the Dummy.*) We can't do anything? Can't you see he's not sane? (*Looks at the Dummy.*) No, no. I'll dash over to see Matveyka. Don't cry, don't cry, you're not well. They'll write you a diagnosis. (*Looks at the Dummy.*) That's it? The visit is over? Thank you.

THE END

PILLOW TALK

by
John Pielmeier

Pillow Talk premiered at the Actors Theatre of Louisville on December 11, 1989. It was directed by V Craig Heidenreich and had the following cast:

MARK ....Josh Liveright
TIFFANY ....Jennifer Marshall
ROGER ....Paul Rogers
JAYDEEN ....Elizabeth Hayward

Production Manager: Bob Krakower
Sound Designer: Mark Hendren
Scenic Designer: Paul Owen
Property Master: Mark Bissonnette
Costume Designer: Melissa Pepper
Lighting Designer: Amy Appleyard
Stage Managers: Mary Czolgosz, Karen Price, Hannah Vesenka
Dramaturg: Mary Samson

CHARACTERS

DOCTOR TIFFANY HEAVEN, 25, a marriage counsellor
MARK BLOOMER, 24, a young newlywed
DOCTOR ROGER CREOSOTE, 26, a marriage counsellor
JAYDEEN BLOOMER, 23, a young newlywed

TIME & PLACE

The marriage counseling room of Creosote and Heaven—no chairs, just lots of big pillows.

  PROP: A battaka

PILLOW TALK

The marriage counseling office of Creosote and Heaven. There is no furniture, just several large pillows suitable for lounging. A battaka, looking like a baseball bat covered in thick cotton batting, lies nearby.
As the LIGHTS rise we see MARK BLOOMER pacing the floor. TIFFANY breezes in.

TIFFANY. Mark? Hi, I'm Doctor Tiffany Heaven. Welcome to Creosote and Heaven. We're so sorry for your pain. Doctor Creosote will be along any moment. Have a pillow. Where's your wife?

MARK. She should be here by now, I'm surprised, she's usually ...

TIFFANY. Is that a noogie?

MARK. What?

TIFFANY. A noogie. A little something she does that gets on your nerves.

MARK. Well, she's usually on time, but for some reason ...

TIFFANY. Use the battaka.

MARK. What?

TIFFANY. (*Handing him the battaka.*) Here. Whenever we encounter the noogies of this life, it's always best to deal with them in a violent and aggressive manner. Hit the pillow and say, "Damn you ..." What's your wife's name?

MARK. Jaydeen.

TIFFANY. Jaydeen. "Damn you, Jaydeen." Say it.

MARK. I don't really ...

TIFFANY. Of course you don't. But you *do*. Inside you *do* want to say it. That's the secret to a happy, healthy, mature relationship. Confront the noogies and slaughter them. Now hit the pillow and say it. "Damn you, Jaydeen."

MARK. Look, this really wasn't my idea, I only came ...

TIFFANY. She made you come to see us, is that what you're saying?

MARK. Well, not exactly *made*, but ...

TIFFANY. Feeling a little castrated, aren't you, Mark? Go with it. Let it out. Hit the pillow and say "I *do* have balls."

MARK. Well ...

TIFFANY. (*Tough as a coach.*) Hit the pillow, Mark! Come on! You want to save this marriage, don't you? Hit the pillow!

MARK. Look, I ...

TIFFANY. You're afraid, is that it? I knew it. You're basically a coward. At bottom you're nothing but a yellow-bellied castrated coward.

MARK. Look, why don't we wait until Jaydeen ...

TIFFANY. Angry, Mark? Does my saying that make you angry? Hit the pillow, Mark! Show me you have balls! Hit the pillow and say "Damn you, Tiffany!"

(*MARK hits the pillow limply.*)

TIFFANY. Say it! "Damn you, Tiffany!"

MARK. Damn you, Tiffany.

TIFFANY. Damn you, Jaydeen!

MARK. (*Hitting the pillow.*) Damn you, Jaydeen!

(*HE continues hitting the pillow as SHE shouts:*)

TIFFANY. That's it! That's it! Oh, that's wonderful! You *do* have balls! You *do* have balls!

MARK. (*Hitting the pillow.*) Damn you, Jaydeen! Damn you, Jaydeen!

(*JAYDEEN enters.*)

JAYDEEN. What the hell did I do now?!

(*MARK stops, nonplussed. TIFFANY is not in the least flustered.*)

TIFFANY. Hi. I'm Doctor Tiffany Heaven. Welcome to Creosote and Heaven. We're so sorry for your pain. Does this bother you, what you just heard? Take the battaka, Jaydeen. Hit the pillow and say "Damn you, Mark." Mark, give her the battaka.

MARK. No.

TIFFANY. Give her the battaka! Don't be hurt by what she's going to say.

MARK. Tell her to get her own battaka.

TIFFANY. (*The angry coach.*) Mark!

(HE surrenders the battaka to TIFFANY, who hands it to JAYDEEN.)

TIFFANY. (*Sweetly.*) Now remember what he said, Jaydeen. He damned you. In front of a total stranger. When he was hitting that pillow he was hitting you. What do you say to that, Jaydeen?

JAYDEEN. Damn you, Mark.

TIFFANY. That's right. Now use the battaka.

JAYDEEN. (*Hits Mark, not the pillow.*) Damn you, Mark! Damn you, Mark!

TIFFANY. The pillow, not your husband!

(JAYDEEN whacks Tiffany with the battaka, knocking her backward into some pillows, then continues her attack on MARK, bringing him to his knees, then to the ground. Breathless, SHE stops, throws the battaka onto the ground, then collapses onto some pillows, exhausted. Silence.)

TIFFANY. (*Sweetly, as if nothing has happened.*) Now ... what seems to be the problem?

(JAYDEEN breaks into sobs, unable to speak. TIFFANY clucks her tongue in disapproval.)

TIFFANY. You did this to her, didn't you, Mark? Oh my.

MARK. I ...

TIFFANY. (*Sadly, sweetly.*) Don't deny it. No one's blaming you. What did you do? Abuse her mentally? Physically? Emotionally? Did you force your big ugly body on her when she didn't want it?

MARK. Look, I ...

TIFFANY. Or was it just the opposite, Mark? Are you incapable of giving her the physical pleasure she so desperately needs?

MARK. No, I ...

TIFFANY. (*Understanding, kind.*) Admit it, Mark. You're a cold-hearted, selfish, shallow individual. Once you admit *that*, your relationship can be saved.

MARK. She's not like this *all* the time ...

TIFFANY. (*Sweetly at first, but the anger of her memories soon overpowers her.*) I used to have a relationship like this too. My first husband chained me to the kitchen stove. Do you believe that? I thought it was normal. I wrote my dissertation on the open oven door. I got a degree in marital counseling and my own personal relationship was a sham. I would have committed suicide if the stove had been gas. I tried to stick my head in the microwave but the chain wouldn't reach. And then I met Roger and I realized that all men weren't like that Neanderthal Hitler I lived with. Just some of them. But *you* can't be helped, Mark. This marriage must *never* be saved. Men like you should be put in jail for what you do to women! You disgust me! Now get out of here! Get the hell out of here before you make me vomit!

MARK. Please, I ...

TIFFANY. (*In an hysterical fury.*) GET OUT! GET OUT!!!

(ROGER enters, breezily.)

ROGER. Sorry I'm late. I'm Doctor Roger Creosote. Welcome to Creosote and Heaven. We're so sorry for your pain.

(ROGER holds out his hand. MARK hesitantly takes it.)

TIFFANY. He's sick, Roger! Sick! Sick! Sick!

ROGER. I see you've met Tiffany.

TIFFANY. Get him out of here!
ROGER. And this must be your lovely wife.
JAYDEEN. (*Looks up at him.*) Roger ...
ROGER. Oh my God ...
TIFFANY. Roger, did you hear me?!

(Sobbing, JAYDEEN runs to Roger, nearly tackling him.)

TIFFANY. What? What is it? Roger, what is she doing?
ROGER. I don't know.
JAYDEEN. Of course you know. I've been waiting for months to talk to you. Why won't you return my calls? Why won't you answer my letters? I can't live another day without you. I only married him because I thought he had your eyes. But on our wedding night he took them out! They were colored contact lenses! And he doesn't make love the way you do! He refuses to do it in the kitchen sink! He says the spigot hurts his back!
TIFFANY. Do you know this woman?
ROGER. Just an old acquaintance, dear.
JAYDEEN. Roger! I love you!

(JAYDEEN kisses him fully on the mouth. ROGER breaks the kiss, with difficulty.)

MARK. Uh, Jaydeen, why didn't you tell me he was ...
TIFFANY. Oh my God! Roger! How could you deceive me like this?!
ROGER. Honestly, Tiffany ...

(JAYDEEN is sobbing, clinging to Roger like poison ivy, kissing his chest, his back, his hands, while ROGER tries to extricate himself.)

MARK. Jaydeen ...
TIFFANY. You set this whole thing up, didn't you?
ROGER. *You* made the appointment.
MARK. Jaydeen, please ...

TIFFANY. You did this just to humiliate me!

ROGER. I swear I didn't know ...

MARK. For better or worse, Jaydeen, remember?

TIFFANY. Oh my God! Throw her out! Kick her out!!!

ROGER. Tiffany, she's hurting.

TIFFANY. She'll be hurting even more when I'm through with her!

(Grabbing the battaka, TIFFANY lunges for the sobbing JAYDEEN. MARK grabs the business-end of the battaka, trying to restrain her.)

MARK. No!

TIFFANY. You stay out of this!

(SHE wrests the battaka from his grasp and hits him, knocking HIM back on the pillows. ROGER gets between her and the sobbing JAYDEEN.)

ROGER. Tiffany, be reasonable. She's never done anything to hurt you. *She's* the one who's suffering. I loved her for a time, and then I met you. We all know that love is a momentary and ephemeral thing. Love changes. She's got to learn that. You do too. We all do.

TIFFANY. Why? What do you mean? What are you trying to say?

ROGER. Love is a wisp on the wind. It blows here, then it blows there ...

TIFFANY. You don't love me anymore? Is that what you're trying to say? You don't love me?!

ROGER. Well, I wouldn't put it quite like that ...

TIFFANY. *(Begins to sob.)* NO!!! No. No. I don't believe this. I don't believe this nightmare!

ROGER. I'm sorry, Tiffany. I'm so sorry for your pain.

TIFFANY. I'll show you pain!

(SHE raises the battaka, and beats Roger several times over the

head with it. JAYDEEN screams. ROGER screams and collapses. MARK tries to pull her back.)

MARK. Hold it! Let's be sensible here!

TIFFANY. You stay out of this!!! (*SHE delivers a couple of battaka blows to Mark, beating him back.*)

JAYDEEN. (*Nurses Roger.*) Oh Roger. Roger.

MARK. (*Warding off the blows.*) Please! I don't mean to get involved here but that's my wife who's ...

(In an instant TIFFANY throws down the battaka and is on Mark, kissing him passionately on the mouth, the eyes. MARK struggles valiantly with her.)

MARK. What are you doing?!

ROGER. Tiffany! Don't!

TIFFANY. (*Breaks the kiss.*) What? Are you jealous? Do you want these kisses, Roger?! Well you can't have them! He's more of a man than you'll ever be!

(TIFFANY kisses Mark again. HE pries away.)

MARK. No, please ...

JAYDEEN. Leave her, Roger. Forget about her. Let's run away.

TIFFANY. You don't need to leave me. *I'm* leaving *you*! *We're* running away, him and me.

MARK. Don't you think we should talk this over ...

TIFFANY. (*Slapping his shoulder.*) You say out of this! (*Then desperately, clinging to Mark, speaking to Roger.*) He loves me, Roger. I'll do anything he wants. I'll be his slave. He'll chain me to the stove and I'll love it!

ROGER. (*Leaping to his feet...*) Stop it! (*...and pulling Tiffany away from Mark.*) Stop it!

(TIFFANY is pleased. For a moment, all is calm.)

ROGER. You're trying to make me jealous, Tiffany, aren't you? Well, it worked. But not the way you think. I don't love you. And I don't love you, Jaydeen. I don't love anybody. I'm a sad, pathetic, despicable human being. We all are. All except this man. (*Putting his arm around Mark.*) The three of us are searching for love and we love no one but ourselves. But this man ... he's good. I sensed it as soon as I walked into the room. He's capable of great affection, great feeling. Aren't you?

MARK. Well, I...

ROGER. And I'm not. I look at a man like this and I am *consumed* with jealousy. (*Fighting emotion, to Mark.*) I could hate you, I could murder you, I could tear you into little pieces and feed you to the dogs, but you know something else? I could also love you. I know I just said I don't love anyone, but if I *could* love anyone, I could love you. (*ROGER falls to his knees, sobbing, laughing, clinging to Mark's knees.*) Yes. Oh yes. I want to love, I want to love *you* and I don't even know your name. I am such a fake! I make money teaching people how to love and I don't even love myself! Help! HELP ME!!! (*ROGER is sobbing, kissing Mark's feet.*)

JAYDEEN. He can't do it, Roger.

MARK. I'm really not that good at loving anyone myself ...

JAYDEEN. He's boring, he's unimaginative ...

TIFFANY. The spigot hurts his back.

JAYDEEN. He's pathetic, he's weak ...

TIFFANY. He's one big noogie.

MARK. I don't love you, Roger!

(*A beat. ROGER looks up.*)

MARK. No offense. Don't take it personally. I can't teach you anything about love because I really don't love *you.*

(*Silence.*)

ROGER. (*Sits back, wipes his eyes, gathers his wits again.*) Well. All right. At least *that's* cleared up.

(Another moment, and then ROGER grabs the battaka and attacks Mark, shouting angry primal screams, beating him to the ground. TIFFANY and JAYDEEN finally succeed in prying Roger away from Mark.)

JAYDEEN. Leave him be, Roger. He's bad for you.
TIFFANY. He's a cold-hearted, selfish, shallow individual. He can't appreciate you, Roger.

(The WOMEN are holding Roger down.)

JAYDEEN. But *we* can. *We* can love you.
TIFFANY. We *do* love you, Roger. And in time, perhaps you can grow to love us.
JAYDEEN. Together.
TIFFANY. We're yours.

(ROGER calms, quietly sobbing. The TWO WOMEN comfort and coo over him, kissing him, loving him, oblivious of Mark.)

MARK. Well ... goodbye then. *(No response.)* I won't be coming back, you know. *(No acknowledgment.)* It's all my fault, I know. And I *do* feel guilty. I guess I just fell in love with the wrong person. *(Nada.)* Life goes on. Right? *(Nope. HE picks up the battaka and playfully hits himself on the head.)* Well ... goodbye.

(No response. Their THREE HEADS are close together, the WOMEN lying on either side of Roger, soothing him. MARK leaves. After a moment HE runs back on, screaming ...)

MARK. NOOGIE!!! *(...battaka still in hand, and brings it down soundly on their three heads. BLACKOUT.)*

THE END

THE PROBLEM-SOLVER

by
Valerie Smith
&
Michael Bigelow Dixon

The Problem-Solver premiered at Actors Theatre of Louisville on December 11, 1989 in an apprentice showcase production. It was directed by Fred Major and had the following cast:

PHIL ....Rob Lanier
MEGAN ....Jennifer Marshall
TINA ....Diane Casey
KURT..Paul Rogers
JER ....Josh Liveright

Production Manager: Bob Krakower
Sound Designer: Mark Hendren
Scenic Designer: Paul Owen
Property Master: Mark Bissonnette
Costume Designer: Melissa Pepper
Lighting Designer: Rob Dillard
Stage Managers: Mary Czolgosz, Karen Price, Hannah Vesenka
Dramaturg: Mary Samson

Subsequently the play was produced at the Lucille Ball Festival of New Comedy, Jamestown, New York in May 1991. It was directed by Roger T. Danforth and had the following cast:

PHIL ....Spike McLure
MEGAN ....Kathryn Rossetter
TINA ....Mary Kane
JER ....Joe White
KURT ....Steve Hofvendahl

CHARACTERS

PHIL, mid-20s, married to Megan
MEGAN, mid-20s, married to Phil
TINA, mid-20s, married to Jer
JER, mid-20s, married to Tina
KURT, mid-20s, friend of Phil's. Not married to anyone.

TIME & PLACE

Summer. A beach house.

THE PROBLEM-SOLVER

Transcendent MORNING SOUNDS. This punctuated by muttered
CURSES and the occasional loud discordant bashing of
METAL. LIGHTS up. A patio with an ocean view. In one area
of the patio, five large rectangular boxes with the word "chair"
stencilled on their sides are stacked. Downstage is a pile of
metal tubing of various lengths, plastic baggies with nuts, bolts,
etc. Each is prominently marked with different letters of the
alphabet. PHIL stands, back to audience, inhaling the ocean
breezes. Occasionally HE turns his head to look in the direction
of the noise which occurs more frequently, increasing in
volume. MEGAN enters.

MEGAN. There you are. What time is it?
PHIL. Six forty-three.
MEGAN. What is all this stuff?

(Offstage GRINDING of a circular saw is heard.)

MEGAN. And what on earth is that racket?
PHIL. I thought it was road construction. Now I m not so sure.
MEGAN. A relaxing vacation, Phil. Our escape from the kids.
No yelling, no crying, no squabbling. No car puzzles with the
pieces missing. No traveling computer games beeping and farting
in our dreams. Just the whoosh-boom of the ocean. The lonely cry
of the gulls, caw-caw.

(High-pitched WHINE of a drill is heard.)

MEGAN. Natural sounds.
PHIL. Hon, it'll be fine. Tina and Jer invited us here and they
promised us peace and quiet. And Kurt will be back to his old self.
Once he unwinds.

MEGAN. I hope so. I don't know if I can take another day like yesterday.

PHIL. Hon, I'm sorry. He's a friend. I thought a break would help him out.

(TINA enters with a kitchen towel and apron. SHE seems edgy, on the verge of tears but puts on a good face.)

TINA. I thought I heard voices. You two are up early. How did you sleep?

(Sound of frenetic HAMMERING on metal.)

PHIL and MEGAN. Fine.

TINA. Is your friend feeling better?

MEGAN. We haven't seen him yet this morning.

TINA. I hope Jer didn't upset him last night.

PHIL. Oh no no no. Now that we're here, Kurt'll be fine. Normally he s a quiet accountant-kind of guy.

MEGAN. Normally he wouldn't throw up in the car.

PHIL. But he's been under a lot of pressure lately, Tina. What with the audit, trying to reconstruct the missing records and everything. You understand.

TINA. I understand.

MEGAN. Failing the lie detector test didn't help.

PHIL. Well, the whole thing has made him a nervous wreck. I hope you don't mind us inviting him along, Tina. Kurt's a good friend.

(Offstage CLANGING.)

MEGAN. Tina, what is that noise?

TINA. That? Oh, that's Jer. He's in the garage putting together the patio furniture. He wanted it to be a surprise. Wants everybody to have breakfast out here so they can enjoy the view. He's been up for hours. You know what a perfectionist he is.

(TINA suddenly wells up, wiping her eyes with her apron.)

PHIL. Tina?
JER. *(Offstage.)* TINA—A—A!
TINA. Better see what he wants. Coffee's on the stove. I'm so happy you're here. *(TINA exits in tears.)*
MEGAN. Coffee?
PHIL. I think so.

(MEGAN starts to exit. KURT enters, red-eyed, rumpled.)

PHIL. 'Morning, Kurt.
KURT. *(Steps on a screwdriver.)* Ouch! Ouch ouch ouch! Get away, you nasty thing! *(Kicks screwdriver.)*
MEGAN. Kurt?
PHIL. He stepped on a screwdriver.
MEGAN. Let me see. Oooo, just a minor puncture. Can't hardly even see it.
KURT. Well it's the blood that gives it away, Megan.
MEGAN. I'll get a Band-aid.
PHIL. Kurt, you've got to take things a little easier, buddy.

(MEGAN exits as TINA enters.)

TINA. *(To offstage.)* All right! All right! I'll find it. *(To Phil and Kurt.)* Oh my. Everybody's up early. Isn't that nice?
KURT. Like my stigmata?
PHIL. Kurt just stepped on a screwdriver.
TINA. Where?
KURT. Here. Sliced into the instep. The most painful part of the foot.
TINA. *(Picking up the screwdriver.)* AHA! *(To offstage.)* Found it! *(TINA exits with screwdriver.)*
KURT. Thank you for your concern.

(MEGAN enters with coffee and Band-aid which SHE gives to

Kurt.)

KURT. This is all wrong, Phil. I should have stayed home and faced the music.

PHIL. Kurt, everything is going to be okay. You just need to rest. Then you can go back fresh, alert, and straighten everything out.

KURT. (*Wincing.*) You're right. You're right. Relax. Rest.

(Sudden sound of offstage DRILL.)

KURT. And we've certainly come to the right place to do that.

MEGAN. Calm down, Kurt.

KURT. You said this place would be quiet.

PHIL. It will be. Okay, so we got off to a rough start. A few more hours in the car than planned. Jer and Tina are really nice people though, Kurt. Jer just says things in a funny way sometimes that's all.

KURT. Funny?!!? Like calling me an imbecile for not being able to read his stupid map.

MEGAN. Kurt, Jer did not call you an imbecile and you know it. All he said was he thought that the turn-off next to the gas station was pretty clearly marked on the map.

KURT. Did it or did it not look like the Big Boy with a hamburg platter? (*Assumes the "Big Boy" pose.*)

PHIL. Well, it could have been a little man with a gas hose like Jer said.

KURT. I don't care. It's a stupid way to indicate a gas station.

(Sound of frenetic HAMMERING.)

KURT. I'm going to crucify that moron with his own Black and Decker!

(Agonizingly high-pitched sound of TEARING METAL under chain-saw.)

MEGAN. I'm sure the noise will stop soon.

(JER enters behind Kurt near end of following speech, disheveled, with drill and hammer in hand, and numerous twisted aluminum tubes under his arms. TINA follows.)

KURT. Oh, I know what you're thinking. Kurt's working himself into another fit. But high-pitched sound waves have been recognized as a form of torture since the Geneva Convention. And people who do this on Saturday mornings are sadists. They're the sick ones! They deserve to die!
MEGAN and PHIL. Mornin', Jer!

(JER walks to the pile of tubing downstage and drops everything. HE then takes an instruction diagram from his pocket and thrusts it in Kurt's face.)

JER. Tell me. What does this say?
KURT. Oh boy, more little pictures. A little screwdriver. Little parts sliding into other little parts. What is it? A little sex manual?
JER. Little pictures. Little, tiny pictures.
TINA. Jer's been working since four. There's been some snags. Don't worry about it sweetheart. Leave it for now.
JER. Little pictures of things that don't happen.
TINA. We can have our breakfast out here anyway.
MEGAN. Right! We use the barstools from the kitchen.
PHIL. Shove some of these boxes together for a table.
JER. Because these are little pictures of things that don't exist.
MEGAN. Ah.
JER. That NEVER existed!
PHIL. Ha! I had the same problem when we bought the gas grill. Remember, Megan?
MEGAN. Yes. Terrible. We finally took it back and exchanged it for the floor model.
TINA. There's an idea. We'll have breakfast out here on the barstools. Then we'll go get the one *they* put together.
JER. *(Retrieves a twisted piece of chrome and waves it around*

dangerously.) See this? See it? I had to cree-ate this. No such piece existed in reality. Yet on the diagram. Look. There it is. See-eeee ...

PHIL, MEGAN, and TINA. Hmmmmmmm.

KURT. Looks like another Big Boy.

JER. Ex-cuse me! I didn't mean to inflict anything on *anyone.* It WAS going to be a surprise. So we could sit out here comfortably. Watch the waves, the birds. Relax.

MEGAN. It was a lovely thought, Jer. Really sweet.

PHIL. It was. And we'll still do it, Jer. Together. What are friends for? Right? We'll whip this pup. Yes, sir.

TINA. Right after breakfast.

KURT. Yes. Food would be nice.

PHIL and MEGAN. Good idea!

JER. You all go on. I'll manage.

TINA. I've made Tina's Special Eggs Benedict. Jer? Your favorite?

JER. I'll have some later.

TINA. It won't be any good later! It's already congealing. Later it will be concrete! Just like last night with that stupid map. And this morning with this stupid, stupid, stupid patio furniture, which is ruining everyone's vacation!

MEGAN. Now, Tina, nobody's vacation is ruined.

TINA. Yes it is! It is! You're having a terrible time!

PHIL. No, now really, it's fine, Tina.

KURT. Well, *I'm* having a terrible time.

PHIL. Tell you what. You go warm up breakfast and we'll all pitch in here. Kurt can *relax* and Jer and I and Megan can snack and assemble. A group effort. Just like the old days. Huh? It'll be fun. Okay?

MEGAN. Tina? Okay?

TINA. Well.

PHIL and MEGAN. That's the spirit!

TINA. Can I reheat mayonnaise?

MEGAN. Sure. It tastes better that way. Phil loves his mayonnaise reheated.

PHIL. Hmmmmmm! Yum! I sure do!

KURT. I just tasted my stomach.

TINA. Oh, I'm really, really glad you two are here. (*TINA exits, sniffing.*)

PHIL. Okay. Jer, where are we?

(*JER hands PHIL the diagram in disgust. During the following exchange, KURT should, in the process of finding a box to sit on, also locate a piece of metal tubing wedged underneath, remove it and twirl it absent-mindedly.*)

MEGAN. You labelled the parts very nicely, Jer.

PHIL. A real professional. No mistaking those parts, eh, Jer? No, sir. Very clear. We have two A's.

MEGAN. Check. There should be two B's.

PHIL. Yep! Two B's.

MEGAN. And one C.

JER. YOU! (*Notices Kurt's piece of tubing, jumps up, and points at it.*)

KURT. ME?!

JER. THAT!

PHIL and MEGAN. WHAT?

JER. WHERE? WHERE DID YOU GET THAT?

KURT. I didn't do anything. It was just laying under the box.

JER. I looked under the box. Over, around, and inside that box. With a microscope. That wasn't there before. I know it wasn't.

KURT. It was right here.

JER. Oh? Really?

KURT. It was. Megan, Phil, you believe me, don't you?

MEGAN and PHIL. (*Dubiously.*) Well ...

JER. That was the piece that was missing. That piece. Right there.

KURT. Oh, well. I confess! I snuck out here in the moonlight and hid it when your back was turned. I've always wanted a bent piece of aluminum tubing. I collect them! And then I sell them to other collectors! For thousands of dollars!

PHIL. Kurt! Jer! Everybody stay calm.

KURT. I'm not ashamed. I saw my opportunity. I took it.

JER. I knew it!

MEGAN. Phil, this is getting out of control.

KURT. He's accusing me of stealing this ... this ... this ... thing! First the audit! Then those idiots with their deceitful little machine. Now this! I don't believe it! Where's the blindfold and cigarette?!

PHIL. Time out! Everybody's tired. Tempers are flaring. Kurt, you go help Tina in the kitchen. We'll get the chair together. Then we'll all go for a nice swim, and everything will be wonderful.

KURT. I didn't steal it!

MEGAN. We know that, Kurt. No one's accusing anyone of stealing anything. Okay? In fact, it's a marvelous thing that you did here. That you, Kurt, found this, the missing piece, because now everything's bound to work. The chair should practically assemble itself now. Right, Phil?

PHIL. Absolutely. Right, Jer?

JER. I suppose.

PHIL and MEGAN. There! You see!

KURT. All right. I'm going. But I'm not a thief!

TINA. (*Enters, tearfully, with smoking frying pan.*) Who borrowed the carving knife?

KURT. This is unbelievable! Give me 'til noon and I'll have every piece of metal in the house!

TINA. All I said was the carving knife was missing. Why is everyone yelling at me! I can't do anything right! Look at the eggs! Ruined! (*SHE begins to cry.*)

KURT. Any ninny knows you can't reheat mayonnaise!!! (*Limps off.*)

MEGAN. Kurt! Please!

TINA. Megan, you said it could be reheated!

(*MEGAN exits with TINA following.*)

MEGAN. (*As THEY go.*) It's OK, Tina, we can scrape away the burnt parts and there'll still be enough mayonnaise for everyone.

JER. He's wound kind of tight, isn't he?

PHIL. Well, Jer, it looks to me like EVERYBODY is wound a little tight.

JER. I looked for that piece, you know.

PHIL. Jer. There's no point continuing here. Let's just call it a day, okay?

JER. You mean give up?

PHIL. Yes.

JER. I'm no quitter, Phil, I'm an engineer. Have been for six years. And during those six years, I've put a lot of things together. Big things. Massive things. With massive problems. And my job has been to solve 'em. It's what I do. What I like to think I do best. So, you want to help me here or not?

PHIL. Okay. But look. Maybe we could just start fresh. A whole new box. A different chair. Come on.

JER. Well ... okay.

(Throughout the following speech, PHIL opens a new box and proceeds to check off various components against the diagram as before.)

JER. See Phil, we're different. You work with people, and there's nothing wrong with that. But sometimes, well, it keeps you from seeing a problem clearly. See, there's a certain Zen process to solving a problem, even a simple problem like a patio chair. The trick is to give it all your attention, to block out distractions. Concentrate. Concentration allows you to visualize first the problem, think it through thoroughly and logically so you can arrive at a complete solution.

(Offstage, the sounds of a DOOR SLAMMING, TINA's hysterical CRYING, a frying pan ricochetting off a wall.)

MEGAN. (*Offstage.*) TEE-NA! That's ENOUGH! Now no more throwing! Give that to me.

TINA. (*Offstage. Simultaneous with above.*) Stupid! Stupid! Stupid!

PHIL. That s great, Jer, but there's no part E in this box.

JER. No E?

PHIL. Or K.

JER. You looked under the box?

PHIL. It isn't here.

(Carrying his luggage, KURT crosses from the house to garage.)

JER. Do you think Kurt ... (took them?)

PHIL. Jer!

MEGAN. *(Appears from house.)* Kurt! Stop acting like a child! Put your suitcase back. Tina, now where are you going? Tina! *(MEGAN exits in direction of house.)*

PHIL. Look. How about we use parts K and E from the first chair to finish this one?

JER. Hey-y, fella! That's using the old noggin.

MEGAN. *(Enters from house and exits into the garage. While passing through, an exasperated whisper.)* Phil!

JER. I wish I hadn't cut and bent that other K.

(Offstage a CAR ENGINE coughs, sputters and then dies.)

PHIL. Well, maybe we don't need a K!

JER. Oh, we definitely need K, Phil. We can't put it together without K. K is vital, see? Sit on this chair without K and you'll need a proctologist.

MEGAN. *(Offstage.)* Kurt! Unlock the door! Well, then roll the window down! Just listen to me for a minute.

(Sound of CAR ENGINE trying to start but sputtering out.)

PHIL. Then maybe we *can* go get the floor model. We put all the pieces back in the box. Wrap 'em up. Take 'em back to Sears and tell 'em it came this way. And then we *make* 'em give us the floor model. Okay?

MEGAN. *(Offstage.)* Kurt!

JER. Nah. Sorry. Can't do that Phil.

(Offstage, sound of CAR ENGINE trying but failing again.)

PHIL. Why not, for God's sake? Why can't we do that?

MEGAN. (*Offstage.*) Kurt! Come on!

JER. Because that's the same as quitting. And like I said I'm a problem-solver, Phil. It's in my blood.

(*During this next speech, MEGAN enters from garage and walks toward house, where she meets TINA, who enters from house with a knife in her hand.*)

MEGAN. Oh, Tina. Good. You found the carving knife.

(*TINA marches past her and exits to garage. MEGAN turns and follows.*)

MEGAN. Now Tina! Kurt! Phil! PHIL! (*Exiting.*) PHIL! PHIL! GET OUT HERE! QUICK!

(*PHIL and MEGAN exit, leaving JER alone to examine the diagram. HE picks up one piece of tubing, compares it to the little picture.*)

JER. Nope. I'm definitely not a quitter.

(*JER pulls out masking tape and begins to tape the pieces that wouldn't fit together with screws. Sounds of ARGUMENT. Sound of CAR revving and peeling out.*)

MEGAN and PHIL. TINA! LOOK OUT! (*Assorted SCREAMS.*) OH MY GOD!

PHIL. Is she okay?

JER. Yup. I m gonna lick this baby, yet.

(*PHIL and MEGAN enter, supporting a wounded, bedraggled TINA between them.*)

PHIL. JER!

MEGAN. JER!

TINA. JER-RRRY!

JER. One moment. Almost done. Ah. Ah. Ah-ha! (*Triumphantly holds up piece taped together.*) This is gonna be one great weekend!

BLACKOUT

THE END

GOLDEN ACCORD

by
Wolę Soyinka

Golden Accord premiered at Actors Theatre of Louisville on February 27, 1980. It was directed by Michael Hankins and had the following cast:

MR. LONESTONE...William McNulty
POLICE SERGEANT ....Dierk Toporzysek
ANNABELLE LONESTONE ....Jeanne Even

Set Design: Paul Owen
Costume Design: Kurt Wilhelm
Lighting Design: Jeff Hill
Co-Property Masters: Sam Garst, Sandra Strawn
Stage Manager: Benita Hofstetter

TIME & PLACE

The action takes place in the living room of the Lonestones, a typical urban apartment in any American big city. Furnishing should be limited to just what is essential in the way of action.

Late evening.

PRODUCTION NOTE

The golden accordion, which is the physical focus of the action, should be a masterpiece of vulgarity, rather like a contracted version of an ornate juke box. When the lid is opened, the interior is rather like a concertina file, stuffed full of notes, lights flashing and winking from every available pore. If it proves possible to incorporate into it a music box of its own, then Mrs. Lonestone, when she makes her last entrance, should not merely turn down the record player but turn if *off* altogether, so that we hear for the first time music from the box itself, which then runs to the end of the action.

GOLDEN ACCORD

FOOTSTEPS and excited VOICES (male) approach the living room of the Lonestones. A KEY is inserted in the door which opens inwards. LONESTONE enters and switches on the light just by the door, then spins round quickly to bar his wife's entrance. HE and the OFFICER speak almost simultaneously.

LONESTONE. Wait. Got to do this properly. (*Sweeps her up in his arms.*)

SERGEANT. And of course there will be a regular patrol all night, just to make sure everything is all right with America's No. 1 Couple.

LONESTONE. (*Carrying his wife over the doorstep.*) 'Cause you see, the first thing we're going to do is have a second honeymoon—anywhere you wish, and that honeymoon begins right now!

SERGEANT. (*Follows into the living room, carrying a gift-wrapped parcel.*) There'll be one of our men to escort you to the bank in the morning.

LONESTONE. (*Standing squarely in the middle of the room, HE tries to kiss his wife but SHE turns her head away.*) Hey, how does it feel to be Mrs. Golden Accord 1980?

ANNABELLE. Will you put me down please?

LONESTONE. What? Oh.

(HE sets her down and ANNABELLE walks straight through another door leading to the bedroom, slams the door.)

SERGEANT. Something bothering the wife?

LONESTONE. Oh you know women. Still upset about me bringing the money home. The studio offered to keep it for us overnight but damnit—if only for one night in my life, I want to go to bed with a hundred and a half grand—yeah, go to sleep and dream of it, then wake up and find it's real!

SERGEANT. Mr. Lonestone, I understand that feeling. (*HE holds out the parcel at arm's length, gazes at it with reverence.*) Wow!

LONESTONE. Oh yes, I'll take that now. May as well start getting used to it.

SERGEANT. Here you are, sir. And my very best wishes to you both.

LONESTONE. Would you mind getting that plug, please? Thank you officer. (*Takes the parcel, look round briefly and settles for an occasional table in the middle of the room, sets the box on the table. Steps back and gazes on it for a moment.*) And this is only the beginning. Wait till we start endorsing products for the big television commercials.

SERGEANT. Yessir! I bet you'll make a little something there, no doubt about it.

LONESTONE. A little something! (*Going towards him.*) Sergeant, ever heard of Pele, the soccer guy?

SERGEANT. Sure. The Latino. Played for Cosmos when he came here.

LONESTONE. Oh, yeah, but he didn't really come to play soccer. His real mission was to sell Pepsi-Cola.

SERGEANT. Ah.

LONESTONE. Well, take Pele, add Mohammed Ali and I'll tell you something—when it comes to money from endorsing products, Mr. & Mrs. Golden Accord (*Tapping himself on chest.*), America's No. 1 Couple are going to prove bigger than both.

SERGEANT. Oh, come now Mr. Lonestone.

LONESTONE. You just mark it down. (*Going to the drinks cabinet.*) From breakfast cereals to family cars, vacation tours ... look, they showed us the list of commercial companies just waiting in the wings. There was even an Opinion Poll Consultancy Firm— got the idea?—"when we want to know what America is thinking, we consult the same opinion poll as America's No. 1 Couple ..."

SERGEANT. I can see you're going to lead a busy life from now on, Mr. Lonestone.

LONESTONE. Getting an agent first thing in the morning. He

can sort out the fat contracts while we enjoy our second honeymoon in the Balearic Islands or some other place. (*HE has taken down a bottle of Canadian Club and some glasses.*) I know you're on duty, sergeant, but ...

SERGEANT. (*Takes off his hat and prepares to be comfortable.*) Matter of fact I'm not, Mr. Lonestone. I was just going off duty when the call came through from the studio, so I volunteered ... well, that's hardly telling the whole story. We all volunteered. Everyone wanted to get close to the lucky pair— maybe some of the luck would rub off.

LONESTONE. Ho ho. Well, what will it be?

SERGEANT. Er ... er ... oh, now I'm embarrassed.

LONESTONE. Embarrassed? What do you want? We've got whisky, beer, sherry ...

SERGEANT. No, it isn't that. It's er ... it's just that there is something I'd like even better than a drink. Just something I want to be able to brag about when I get back to the station tomorrow. If you wouldn't really mind, Mr. Lonestone.

LONESTONE. Well, spell it out man. What is it? You want my autograph?

SERGEANT. No, though I wouldn't mind that too. But ... if you wouldn't mind, could you ... open ... while I'm here. (*Pointing to the box.*) I've never seen a hundred and fifty thousand dollars in real life, much less handled it.

LONESTONE. (*A slow grin spreading over his face, erupts suddenly into a thigh-slapping roar of laughter.*) Well I'll be damned... if you only knew what had been going through my mind! As soon as you left I was going to open up that golden box, strip stark naked and scrub myself from head to crotch with those stacks of bills. (*Excitement mounting.*) Come on, get the damned thing out in the open air. Must be getting suffocated in there. Wait a minute, wait a minute, this needs some champagne. There must be a couple of bottles in the fridge. You get to work on the wrapping while I hunt down the champagne!

ANNABELLE. (*Appears in the bedroom doorway.*) Do you mind? The children are trying to sleep.

LONESTONE. To hell with that. Tell them to come out and

celebrate. Christ! Is this a night for sleeping?

ANNABELLE. What are they supposed to celebrate, Lonestone?

LONESTONE. (*Hesitates. THEY hold each other's gaze for a moment.*) Oh get back to sleep yourself Mrs. Wet Blanket 1980. (*HE dashes towards the refrigerator, rummages within and hauls out one, then two bottles of champagne.*)

SERGEANT. Perhaps I ought to go. I could come back later.

LONESTONE. Nonsense. Take off the wrapping. When she sets her eyes on those hundred-dollar bills she'll feel different. Wait, something is missing. Music. We should have some music.

(*ANNABELLE turns back into the bedroom. SERGEANT hesitates, then begins feverishly to unwrap the box.*)

LONESTONE. Now what would be appropriate for an occasion like this? A hundred and fifty thousand dollar composition. Do you enjoy classical music, officer? (*HE is shoving aside one disc after another as he talks.*) Damn! I used to have Tchaikovsky's 1812 in my collection. All those cannon booms and church bells—Ah-ha, this will do I think. What do you think of the sound-track to that fantastic space film—2001? Yeah, absolutely perfect. It's like being launched in space you know—spaced OUT—Man, with a hundred and fifty thousand sitting in my living room, who needs drugs?

SERGEANT. (*Has untied the strings and removed the wrappers. The strains of Strauss' Thus Spak Zarathustra envelop the scene. HE steps back from the table.*) Undo the clasp please, Mr. Lonestone.

(*LONESTONE, still on his knees by the record player, turns toward the table. HIS eyes light on the shiny metallic box sitting in a cloud of chiffon paper wrappings. Picking up the champagne bottle, HE begins to crawl towards the table on both knees.*)

LONESTONE. I did it. Oh my God, you mean, I actually did

it?

SERGEANT. Oh yes Mr. Lonestone, it took guts but you did it. You and your wife.

LONESTONE. Just look at it. I call that poetry. Music.

SERGEANT. Lonestone.

LONESTONE. The clasp. Oh yes, in a minute. (*HE eases the cork off the champagne bottle, pops it and sprays the frothing liquid all over the box. With his other hand HE quickly releases the clasp of the box. The vertical lid falls slowly down, revealing a concertina-like interior from which stacks of dollar bills fan outwards.*)

SERGEANT. Style. If there is one thing that programme has, it is—style.

LONESTONE. (*Gently plucking out a stack of notes. Holds it up and raises the champagne bottle.*) To the sweet notes of the Golden Accord. (*Drinks and passes the bottle to the Sergeant.*)

(*ANNABELLE reenters, takes in the scene, then comes forward to the table so that she is standing behind it, overlooking both the box and Lonestone on the down side of the table.*)

ANNABELLE. (*Quietly.*) The children just woke up.

LONESTONE. (*His gaze does not swerve from the box.*) I said bring them out to join the fun.

ANNABELLE. I don't think they want to join the fun.

LONESTONE. Why the hell not?

ANNABELLE. They watched the programme.

LONESTONE. Then they must know that their father is one hundred and fifty thousand, seven hundred and fifty dollars richer than he was when he left the house this evening.

ANNABELLE. Yes. They heard their father's answer to the question: What is the most shameful secret your wife ever confided in you?

(*A brief silence. LONESTONE raises his head to meet his WIFE's unsmiling face. The POLICEMEN takes a step away from the table, turning his head away. HE moves progressively further*) *as if trying to place himself out of earshot.)*

LONESTONE. Well, then they must also have heard their mother confirm the story when it came to her turn.

ANNABELLE. Would there have been any point in denying it?

LONESTONE. We agreed before we set out—no lies. Wasn't that the deal?

ANNABELLE. Oh yes. Does your husband snore in bed? Who does the washing up in your home? Is your wife a slob around the house? That sort of question was all we had in mind. You are not an honest man if you claim otherwise, Lonestone. What is the most shameful secret your wife ever confided in you—and you told.

LONESTONE. A deal is a deal. What are you beefing about anyway? That was the jackpot question. We were way up in front of the other couples—what was the point throwing it all away on account of some silly sensitivity?

ANNABELLE. No one ever told you that the secrets of the bedroom are as sacred as those of the confessional?

LONESTONE. Yeah? What century are you thinking of? Come off it woman.

ANNABELLE. Well, to tell you the truth, I had this same century in mind. You know, this same one from which you received twelve years of my life, of my body. Twelve years nursing your frustrations, your miseries and weaknesses in the privacy of my strength, and bearing you three children.

LONESTONE. (*Getting up.*) Look, you keep your mind on the money ...

ANNABELLE. I do have my mind on the money.

LONESTONE. Good. I mean, what else could have been on it when it came to your turn? Damnit, you got the same question didn't you? What is the most shameful secret you ever confided in your husband—eh?—Mrs. Lonestone? And you told.

ANNABELLE. I saw your face. It was there. The whole studio reeked of it. The other couples in the competition, the studio audience, even the ones I couldn't see, the millions of strangers wallowing in the secret mess I thought I had buried safely with you. Yes, I thought then of the money ...

LONESTONE. Who cares when you thought of it? You backed up the truth, we qualified for the Perfect Accord between husband and wife and here we are—overnight celebrities, a hundred and fifty grand richer, so cut out the belly-aching!

ANNABELLE. Have you ever watched yourself die, Lonestone?

LONESTONE. What's that?

ANNABELLE. Because that was what happened to me tonight. After I read my betrayal on your face, those studio lights burnt right through into my brain, and I felt myself shrivel and die. Do you know what that is like?

LONESTONE. (*Offhand.*) No, tell me.

ANNABELLE. Actually I don't believe you are listening to me, Lonestone.

LONESTONE. Sure I am. You said you watched yourself shrivel and die—okay? (*HE gathers up a fistful of notes and thrusts them under her nose.*) Get a whiff of that. Nothing like it for reviving the dead.

ANNABELLE. (*Produces a gun from her pocket and levels it at him.*) I have thought about this all evening: I wasn't sure I could bring myself to do it but ... now I think I shall actually enjoy it.

LONESTONE. (*His eyes incredulous on the gun.*) What ... what is that for?

SERGEANT. (*Turns, hand to his holster.*) For God's sake Mrs. Lonestone!

ANNABELLE. Do what you like Sergeant. As long as you know I'm making sure of him.

LONESTONE. (*Backing off.*) Now wait Annabelle, just wait a minute ...

ANNABELLE. Don't move one step further Lonestone.

LONESTONE. (*Stops dead.*) No, I'm not moving, I'm not moving Annabelle. Just listen to me a minute.

ANNABELLE. You are alone with your death, Lonestone. Just you and your death. It is rather late in the day but maybe you now understand what a private moment means ... just you, and your death. Try and savor it—if you can.

SERGEANT. Mrs. Lonestone, please don't make me draw. Put

down that gun.

LONESTONE. You can have all the money, Annabelle. I'll sign it over to you. It's all yours ... everything ... the Sergeant can witness it ...

ANNABELLE. What money? It's all gone on legal defense. The jury will be sympathetic but lawyers still cost money.

SERGEANT. I'm warning you Mrs. Lonestone. If you don't put that thing down ...

ANNABELLE. Don't be a fool, officer. My husband taught me how to use this gun.

LONESTONE. Think of the children for God's sake! Look, I'll leave the house tonight, never come back. Anything you want ...

ANNABELLE. Good-bye Lonestone.

(*SHE presses the trigger. There is a CLICK but no explosion. LONESTONE raises his arms instinctively to ward off impact. The SERGEANT draws his gun and covers Annabelle.*)

SERGEANT. Drop it!

ANNABELLE. (*Lets the gun dangle from a finger, lowers her arm.*) It's empty. I unloaded it myself. (*SHE replaces the gun in her pocket, moves toward the bedroom. Stops and turns to the Sergeant.*) Remember to take that—(*Indicating her husband.*) thing with you when you leave.

THE END

LAST DAY OF CAMP

by
Jeffrey Sweet

Last Day of Camp premiered at the Actors Theatre of Louisville on June 5, 1989. It was directed by J. Christopher Wineman and had the following cast:

CRAIG ....David Burke
LILLIAN ....Sharyn Jensen
FIONA ....Judith Rothberg

Scenic Designer: Paul Owen
Sound Designer: Mark Hendren
Property Master: Mark Bissonnette
Production Stage Manager: Carey Upton
Costume Designer: Kevin McLeod
Lighting Designer: Jan Thornsberry
Technical Director: Steve Goodin
Production Managers: Bob Krakower, J. Christopher Wineman
Dramaturg: Sonja Kuftinec

CHARACTERS

CRAIG
LILLIAN
FIONA

TIME & PLACE

The play takes place outside, at a camp, near the end of summer.

LAST DAY OF CAMP

LILLIAN and CRAIG relaxing.

CRAIG. They do twinkle.

LILLIAN. Isn't that amazing? They really do.

CRAIG. You didn't know that?

LILLIAN. Not really.

CRAIG. Come on, you must know the song. Everybody knows the song.

LILLIAN. Which?

CRAIG "Twinkle, Twinkle, Little Star." You don't know that?

LILLIAN. Sure.

CRAIG. Where do you think they got that from? I mean, art imitates life, right?

LILLIAN. I don't know. There's a lot of bullshit in songs. The only stars I ever saw twinkle were in Disney cartoons or Christmas pageants. Till this summer. I guess it's pretty hard to twinkle through all that guck in the city.

CRAIG. So you've had an educational summer, hunh?

LILLIAN. You're laughing at me.

CRAIG. Not really.

LILLIAN. That's OK.

CRAIG. I'm not laughing.

LILLIAN. You aren't?

CRAIG. No

LILLIAN. I'm glad. But it would have been OK if you were. I mean, I like you.

CRAIG. Well, that goes both ways. And I wasn't laughing at you.

LILLIAN. (*Pretending to be embarrassed.*) Well, gosh and shucks, Craig. (*A beat.*) So quiet now. I've gotten so used to hearing kids' voices. Now they're gone, it all sounds sort of naked.

275

CRAIG. You packed?

LILLIAN. I'm putting it off.

CRAIG. I know, it's a drag, isn't it?

LILLIAN. No, it's not that. I think I just don't want to admit that it's over.

(FIONA enters.)

FIONA. Well, Lucy Bernell's mother finally showed up.

CRAIG. About time.

LILLIAN. What's this about?

FIONA. One of my little monsters in cabin three. Her mother was supposed to pick her up and she was late or something.

CRAIG. The mother or the kid?

FIONA. Who cares? They're both gone and out of our hair. They're all gone, thank God.

LILLIAN. You really like kids, don't you?

FIONA. Let's just say that when it comes to Hansel and Gretel, my sympathies are with the witch.

LILLIAN, Which is why of course you took a job in a summer camp.

FIONA. I heard there was a lake here. Thought with luck I might see one drown.

CRAIG. What a pleasant thought.

FIONA. I'm a meanie, didn't you know that?

CRAIG. Sure.

FIONA. I am.

CRAIG. I believe you.

FIONA. OK, don't say I didn't warn you.

CRAIG. Guess what I got for a tip?

FIONA. Most I got was a twenty.

LILLIAN. That's not bad.

FIONA. It's OK, but nothing spectacular. Divide that down by the hours I spent making sure they didn't break an ankle or get eaten by a bear, comes to pretty cheap babysitting.

LILLIAN. What were you saying, Craig?

CRAIG. This guy hands me an envelope and right away I can

feel there's something other than money in it. I open it up and it's maybe an ounce of grass.

LILLIAN. Whose daddy was that?

CRAIG. You know Dave Greenberg?

FIONA. The little freak?

CRAIG. A clear case of like son, like father.

FIONA. OK, let's see.

CRAIG. See what?

FIONA. Isn't he cute when he plays innocent? Your tip.

CRAIG. I'll show you mine if you show me yours.

FIONA. You know what I'll bet, I'll bet it's some of that anemic home-grown stuff.

CRAIG. Only one way to find out.

FIONA. All right then, break it out and let's put it to the test.

CRAIG. Don't have it with me.

FIONA. Where is it?

CRAIG. Back in my cabin, in my secret hiding place.

FIONA. I'll bet.

LILLIAN. You'll want to be careful.

CRAIG. What about?

LILLIAN. Remember what happened to Leonard.

CRAIG. Leonard was a different case entirely.

LILLIAN. They caught him with dope.

CRAIG. They caught him turning on the kids in his cabin. That was Leonard's fatal mistake.

FIONA. Yeah, but till they kicked him out, he was the most popular counselor in the camp.

CRAIG. I think what tipped them off was the water pipe one of his kids made in arts and crafts.

LILLIAN. I'm just saying be careful.

CRAIG. I appreciate your concern. But we're leaving tomorrow, so it's not like there's any great danger.

FIONA. You going to turn him in, Lillian?

LILLIAN. Of course not. Why would you say a thing like that?

FIONA. Maybe you don't approve.

LILLIAN. It's not a matter of my approving or disapproving ...

FIONA. She said disapprovingly.

LILLIAN. It's not. Just because I don't do it, I'm not laying anything on anyone else.

CRAIG. You've never smoked?

LILLIAN. Sure, I've smoked, but not anymore.

FIONA. Got to protect those chromosomes.

LILLIAN. No, it's just I didn't enjoy it.

CRAIG. You're kidding.

LILLIAN. Why am I kidding?

CRAIG. You didn't enjoy it at all?

LILLIAN. What, is this the new taboo—you don't admit you don't enjoy dope? You say it like it's something I should be ashamed of.

CRAIG. No.

LILLIAN. If you enjoy it, terrific.

CRAIG. Well, I do.

LILLIAN. Terrific. It's not often you find something you really enjoy. Only we all enjoy different things. If we didn't, what would be the point of being different people?

FIONA. Bet you I know why you don't like dope.

LILLIAN. I just don't.

FIONA. It scares you.

LILLIAN. No.

FIONA. You feel those inhibitions slipping away, you're afraid of what you might do. What wild, disgraceful things you might do. Maybe dance or tell dirty jokes or take your clothes off.

LILLIAN. I can do all those things without smoking.

FIONA. Yeah, but *do* you?

LILLIAN. Is that what you think of me—that I'm some virginal square hard-ass?

FIONA What I think is you're a lady who hasn't investigated her full potential for having a good time.

LILLIAN. OK, yeah, right. There you have me nailed into one pithy sentence.

FIONA. Just telling you what I see.

LILLIAN. Thank you very much.

FIONA. OK, take it the wrong way if you want to.

LILLIAN. Don't you worry about what kind of time I'm

having.

FIONA. OK.

LILLIAN. I'm having a fine time.

FIONA. If you say so.

(A beat.)

CRAIG. So what about it?

FIONA. What?

CRAIG. You want to sample a little of my tip?

FIONA. I thought you said you didn't have it with you.

CRAIG. Not with me, but back at my cabin.

FIONA. Back at your cabin, hunh?

CRAIG. Well, that's where it is.

FIONA. In your secret hiding place.

CRAIG. Yes.

FIONA. Back in your cabin.

CRAIG. Right.

FIONA. Well, it's a tempting offer, but no, I don't think so.

CRAIG. No, hunh?

FIONA. Mind you I'm flattered ...

CRAIG. Nothing to be flattered. Just had a little, thought I might share with an appreciative colleague.

FIONA. I see.

CRAIG. That's all that was on my mind. Honest.

FIONA. You're getting cute again.

CRAIG. Well then, maybe back in the city, hunh?

FIONA. You're almost irresistible when you're cute.

CRAIG. So?

FIONA. I said "almost."

CRAIG. You're a cruel woman, Fiona.

FIONA. I told you I was. You thought I was lying, didn't you?

CRAIG. Oh well, guess I'll just have to smoke it myself.

FIONA. You could always look up Leonard. I'm sure he'd be glad to help you out.

CRAIG. Cruel.

FIONA. Goodnight.

LILLIAN. Night.

(FIONA exits.)

CRAIG. See how nuts she is about me?

LILLIAN. No accounting for taste.

CRAIG. Meaning me or her?

LILLIAN. Meaning nothing in particular really.

CRAIG. No, what, do you think I'm crazy?

LILLIAN. I don't know what to think.

CRAIG. Come on, Lil, we're friends. You can call me an asshole if you think I am one.

LILLIAN. I just don't think there's much potential there. For all of her talk about relaxing inhibitions and stuff, I don't think she ...

CRAIG. What ?

LILLIAN. No, I feel stupid talking about her like this.

CRAIG. What were you going to say?

LILLIAN. Just I don't think there's much action behind the talk.

CRAIG. Well, it isn't all talk.

LILLIAN. No?

CRAIG. No.

LILLIAN. How do you know?

CRAIG. Well, it happens I do know.

LILLIAN. You and she?

CRAIG. Once.

LILLIAN. Oh.

CRAIG. A couple weeks ago.

LILLIAN. How about that?

CRAIG. You don't mind me talking about this?

LILLIAN. Why should I mind?

CRAIG. It's just ...

LILLIAN. You're pretty stuck on her, hunh?

CRAIG Yeah, and I sort of got the impression that night that it was mutual. Or maybe I was reading something into it. Seeing what I wanted to see.

LILLIAN. That can happen.

CRAIG. Oh well, I guess I'll get over it. I mean, I was still in the infatuation stage. It really hadn't taken root.

LILLIAN. Not enough time.

CRAIG. Probably. Though this switch on her part, I guess it's got me a little off-balance. I mean, if she wasn't interested, then what was that night all about?

LILLIAN. Maybe she just wanted a good piece of ass.

CRAIG. (*Laughs.*) Anything's possible.

(THEY lean back a minute.)

LILLIAN. (*Sings.*)
"Twinkle, twinkle, little bat,
How I wonder what you're at."

CRAIG. Where'd you hear that?

LILLIAN. I think it's out of Lewis Carroll. That or *Pogo*. I'm not sure. (*Sings.*)
"Up above the world so high,
Like a tea-tray in the sky."

(*Speaks.*) Lewis Carroll.

(A beat.)

CRAIG. Hey.

LILLIAN. What?

CRAIG. What do you say, in five years, if you aren't married and I'm not married, we get together and talk about it?

LILLIAN. What?

CRAIG. I'm not saying do it necessarily. But talk about it. And who knows, maybe do it. We could both probably do a lot worse, and probably will. So, what do you say? Five years?

(A beat.)

LILLIAN. (*Trying to hide how upset SHE is.*) You can be very cruel, you know that?

CRAIG. What? What did I say?

LILLIAN. Never mind. (*SHE gets up.*)
CRAIG. Where you going?
LILLIAN. I really ought to pack.
CRAIG. No, wait, hold on.

(*HE reaches out for her. SHE moves away from him, begins to cry.*)

CRAIG. What is it? Please.
LILLIAN. You stupid asshole.
CRAIG. (*Now HE understands.*) I'm sorry.
LILLIAN. You stupid, stupid asshole. (*SHE runs off.*)

THE END

EUKIAH

by
Lanford Wilson

Eukiah is the co-winner of the Actors Theatre of Louisville 1991 National Ten-Minute Play Contest and the Heideman Award.

Eukiah premiered at the Actors Theatre of Louisville on June 17, 1991. It was directed by Marcia Dixcy and had the following cast:

BUTCH...Arthur Aulisi
EUKIAH..Jim Dubensky

Scenic Design: Paul Owen
Lighting Design: Matt Reinert
Costume Designer: Kevin McLeod
Sound Designer: Darron West
Property Master: Mark Bissonnette
Production Manager: Bob Krakower
Stage Manager: Emily Fox
Dramaturg: Emily F. Morse

CHARACTERS:

BUTCH
EUKIAH

TIME & PLACE

The present.
Abandoned, private airplane hangar.

EUKIAH

*A DARK empty stage represents a long abandoned private
airplane hangar. The space is vast and almost entirely dark. A
streak of LIGHT from a crack in the roof stripes the floor.*
*BUTCH walks into the light. HE is a young powerful, charming
man; everybody's best friend. HE is also menacing. Nothing he
says is introspective. Everything is for a purpose. During the
indicated beats of silence he listens; for Eukiah to answer, for
the sound of breathing, for the least indication of where Eukiah
is. The play is a seduction.*

Voices have a slight ECHO in here.

BUTCH. Eukiah? (*Beat.*) Eukiah? (*Beat.*) Barry saw you run in
here, so I know you're here. You're doin' it again, Eukiah, you're
jumping to these weird conclusions you jump to just like some
half-wit. You don't wanna be called a half-wit, you gotta stop
actin' like a half-wit, don't ya? You're gettin' to where nobody can
joke around you, ya know that? What kind of fun is a person like
that to be around, huh? One you can't joke around? We talked
about that before, remember? (*Beat.*) Eukiah? What're you
thinkin'? You thinkin' you heard Barry say something, you
thought he meant it, didn't you? What did you think you heard?
Huh? What'd you think he meant? Eukiah? (*Beat.*) You're gonna
have to talk to me, I can't talk to myself here. (*Beat.*) Have you
ever known me to lie to you? Eukiah? Have you ever known that?
(*Pause. HE might walk around some.*) Okay. Boy, this old hangar
sure seen better days, hasn't it? Just like everything else on this
place, huh? Been pretty much a losing proposition since I've
known it, though. Probably you too, hasn't it? Hell, I don't think
they have the wherewithal anymore, give even one of those ol'
barns a swab a paint. You think? Might paint 'em pink, whattaya

285

think? Or candy stripes. Red and white. Peppermint. You'd like
that. (*Beat.*) This'll remind you of old Mac's heyday, though,
won't it? Private airplane hangar. Talk about echoes, this is an
echo of the past, huh? Ol' Mac had some winners, I guess, about
twenty years ago. That must have been the life, huh? Private
planes, keep 'em in your private hangar. You got your luncheons
with the dukes and duchesses. Winner's Circle damn near every
race. If they wasn't raised by Ol' Mac or their sire or dam one
wasn't raised by Ol' Mac, I don't imagine anybody'd bother to bet
on 'em, do you? Boy that's all gone, huh? Planes and limos and all,
dukes and duchesses—good lookin' horses, though. Damn shame
we can't enter 'em in a beauty contest somewhere. I know, you're
attached to 'em, but I'll tell you they make damn expensive pets.

What was you? Out by the paddock when Barry was talkin' to
me? You think you overheard something, is that it? What do you
think you heard? You want to talk about it? I know you'd rather
talk to me than talk to Barry, huh? Eukiah? (*Pause.*) Is this where
you come? When you run off all temperamental and sulking?
Pretty nasty old place to play in. Echoes good though. Gotta keep
awful quiet if you're trying to be secret like you always do in a
place like this.

Why do you do that? You got any idea? I'm serious, now. Run
off like that. They're waitin' supper on you, I guess you know.
You know how happy they're gonna be about it, too. (*Beat.*)
Eukiah? What was it you think you heard, honey? What? Was it
about horses? 'Cause I thought I told you never trust anything
anybody says if it's about horses.

EUKIAH. (*Still unseen.*) I heard what Barry said. You said you
would, too.

BUTCH. (*Relaxes some, smiles.*) Where the dickens have you
got to? There's so much echo in here I can't tell where you are.
You back in those oil drums? You haven't crawled up in the rafters
have you? Watch yourself. We don't want you gettin' hurt. I don't
think those horses would eat their oats at all, anybody gave 'em to
'em 'cept you. I think they'd flat out go on strike. Don't you
figure?

EUKIAH. They wouldn't drink, you couldn't get 'em to.

BUTCH. Don't I know it. Pot-A-Gold, for sure. You're the only one to get him to do anything. I think he'd just dehydrate. He'd blow away, you wasn't leadin' him. We could lead him to water but we couldn't make him to drink, isn't that right? (*Beat.*) What are you hiding about? Nobody's gonna hurt you. Don't I always take up for you? You get the weirdest ideas. What do you think you heard Barry say?

EUKIAH. He's gonna burn the horses.

BUTCH. What? Oh, man. You are just crazy sometimes, these things you dream up. Who is? Barry? What would he wanna do something crazy like that for?

EUKIAH. I heard you talkin'.

BUTCH. Can you answer me that? What would he even dream of doin' something like that?

EUKIAH. For the insurance.

BUTCH. No, Eukiah. Just come on to supper, now, I got a date tonight, I can't mess around with you anymore. You really are a half-wit. I'm sorry, but if you think Barry'd do something like that, I'm sorry, that's just flat out half-witted thinkin'. It's not even funny. The way you talk, you yak all day to anybody around, no idea what you're saying half the time; anybody heard something like that there wouldn't be no work for me or you or anybody else around here, 'cause they just lock us all up.

EUKIAH. You said you would.

BUTCH. *I* would? I would what?

EUKIAH. You said it was about time somebody did somethin'.

BUTCH. Eukiah, come out here. I can see you over by that old buggy, my eyes got used to the dark. There ain't no sense in hiding anymore. (*Beat.*) Come on out, damnit, so we can go to supper. I'm not going to play with you anymore. Come on. Well, just answer me one thing. How's burnin' 'em up gonna be any better than maybe splittin' a hoof or somethin' like that? Come on, crazy. The least little thing happens to make a horse not run, it's the same as if he had to be destroyed, you ought to know that.

(*EUKIAH is just visible now. HE is maybe sixteen years old. HE is
    slow and soft; he has the mentality of an eight-year-old.*)

EUKIAH. Yeah, but they already took Pot-A-Gold and Flashy and that gray one, the speckled one, off. They already sold 'em.

BUTCH. Which one do you call Flashy, you mean Go Carmen? The filly? And Old Ironside? Why would they do that?

EUKIAH.'Cause they're the best ones. Then they put three no good horses in their stalls, so nobody would know. And they're gonna burn 'em and nobody can tell they ain't the horses they're supposed to be, Butchy.

BUTCH. Nobody could run Pot-A-Gold somewhere else, Euky. You know those numbers they tattoo in his mouth? That's gonna identify him no matter where he goes, anybody'll know that's Pot-A-Gold.

EUKIAH. Some other country. They wouldn't care.

BUTCH. Anywhere on earth ...

EUKIAH. They got some plan where it'll work, 'cause I heard 'em.

BUTCH. I don't know what you think you heard, but you're really acting half-witted here.

EUKIAH. Don't call me—

BUTCH. Well, I'm sorry, but what would you call it? A person can't burn down a barn full of horses, Euky. What a horrible thing to think. No wonder you get scared, you scare yourself thinking things like that. Those horses are valued, hell I don't even know, millions of dollars probably. Insurance inspectors come around, they take a place apart. You tell me, how would somebody get away with a trick like that?

EUKIAH. What was you talkin' about then?

BUTCH. I don't even know. Where it was you heard what you thought you heard. You're too fast for me. You'll just have to go into supper and ask Mac what Barry was talking about, won't you? Would that make you feel better? Instead of jumpin' to your weird conclusions. Now, can you get that out of your head? Huh? So we can go eat and I can take a bath and go on my date? Is that all right with you? Then I'll come back and tell you all about it. Got a date with Mary, you'd like to hear about that, wouldn't you?

(EUKIAH begins to grin.)

BUTCH. Yes? That's okay with you, is it?

EUKIAH. I guess. *(HE moves into the light, closer to Butch.)*

BUTCH. You guess. You're just going to have to trust me, Eukiah, nobody needs money that bad. Not even on this place. I don't even think nobody could get away tryin' to pull something like that.

(HE puts his arm around Eukiah's neck and THEY start to move off, but BUTCH has Eukiah in a head lock. HE speaks with the strain of exertion.)

BUTCH. Not unless there was some half-wit on the place that got his neck broke being kicked in the head and got burned up in the fire.

(EUKIAH goes to his knees. BUTCH bears down on his neck; it breaks with a dull snap. HE lets EUKIAH slump to the floor. BUTCH is breathing hard, standing over Eukiah's body.)

BUTCH. I thought I told you. Never trust anything anybody says if it's about horses.

THE END

Other Publications for Your Interest

MOVIE OF THE MONTH
(COMEDY)
By DANIEL MELTZER

2 men—Interior

This new comedy by the author of the ever-popular *The Square Root of Love* is an amusing satire of commercial television. B.S., a TV programming executive, is anxious to bolster his network's ratings, which have been sagging of late due to programming disasters such as a documentary called "The Ugly Truth" (says B.S.: "What the hell is The Ugly Truth, and how the hell did it get into our Prime Time?") His eagerbeaver assistant, appropriately named Broun, has found a script which he is sure can be made into a hit "Movie of the Month". It's about this Danish prince, see, who comes home from college to find that his uncle has murdered his father and married his mother . . . Well, naturally, B.S. has his own ideas about how to fix such a totally unbelievable plot . . .   (#17621)

SUNDANCE
(ALL GROUPS—COMEDY)
By MEIR Z. RIBALOW

5 men—Simple interior

This new comedy from the author of *Shrunken Heads* is set in a sort of metaphysical wild west saloon. The characters include Hickock, Jesse, the Kid, and the inevitable Barkeep. Hickock kills to uphold the law. Jesse kills for pleasure. The Kid kills to bring down The Establishment. What if, wonders the Barkeep, they met up with the Ultimate Killer—who kills for no reason, who kills simply because that's what he does? Enter Sundance. He does not kill to uphold the law, for pleasure, or to make a political statement, or because he had a deprived childhood. And he proceeds to kill everyone, exiting at the end with his sixguns blazing! "Witty, strong, precise, unusually well-written."—The Guardian. "A brilliant piece."—Dublin Evening Press. This co-winner of the 1981 Annual NYC Metropolitan Short Play Festival has been a success in 6 countries!   (#3113)

Other Publications for Your Interest

ADVICE TO THE PLAYERS
(DRAMA)

By BRUCE BONAFEDE

5 men, 1 woman (interracial)—Interior

Seldom has a one-act play created such a sensation as did *Advice to the Players* at Actors Theatre of Louisville's famed Humana Festival of New American Plays. Mr. Bonafede has crafted an ingenious play about two Black South African actors, here in America to perform their internationally-acclaimed production of *Waiting for Godot.* The victims of persecution in their own country, here in the U.S. they become the victims of a different kind of persecution. The anti-apartheid movement wants a strong political gesture—they want the performance cancelled. And, they are willing to go to any lengths to achieve this aim—including threatening the families of the actors back home. Cleverly, Mr. Bonafede juxtaposes the predicament of Didi and Gogo in *Waiting for Godot* with the predicament of the two actors. Both, in an odd, ironic way, are Theatre of the Absurd. "A short play blazing with emotional force and moral complexities . . . taut, searing inquiry into the inequities frequently perpetrated in the name of political justice . . . a stunning moment of theatrical truth."—Louisville Courier-Journal.   (#3027)

APPROACHING LAVENDAR
(COMIC DRAMA)

By JULIE BECKETT CRUTCHER

3 women—Interior

While their father is marrying his fourth wife sardonic, controlled Jenny and her slightly neurotic housewife-sister Abigail wait in a church vestibule. There they encounter Wren, the spacey ingenue who is about to become their step-sister. The mood of polite tolerance degenerates with comic results as inherent tensions mount and the womens' conflicted feelings about their parents' remarriage surface. The contingent self-discovery results in new understanding and forgiveness, and ultimately reveals the significance of sisterhood. Highly-praised in its debut at the famed Actors Theatre of Louisville, the play was singled out by the Louisville press for its "precise and disquieting vision" as well as its sharp humor, as it "held a capacity audience rapt."   (#3649)

A TANTALIZING
(DRAMA)

By WILLIAM MASTROSIMONE

1 man, 1 woman—Interior

Originally produced by the amazing Actors Theatre of Louisville, this is a new one-act drama by the author of *The Woolgatherer* and *Extremities. A Tantalizing* is about the attempts by a young woman to "save" a street bum, a tattered and crazy old man whom she has dragged in off the street. Like Rose in *Extremities* she, too, has secrets in her closet. What these secrets are is the intriguing mystery in the plot of the play, as we gradually realize why the woman has taken such an interest in the bum.   (#22021)

Other Publications for Your Interest

PASTORAL
(COMEDY)

By PETER MALONEY

1 man, 1 woman—Exterior

Daniel Stern ("Blue Thunder", "Breaking Away") and Kristin Griffith ("The Europeans", "Interiors") starred originally at NYC's famed Ensemble Studio Theatre in the preceptive comedy about a city couple temporarily tending a farm. He hates the bucolic life and is terrified, for instance, by such horrors as a crowing rooster; whereas she is at one with the land *and* the rooster. "An endearing picture of young love at a comic crossroads."—N.Y. Times. "Sharp, satiric humor."—New Yorker. "An audience pleaser."—Village Voice. Published with *Last Chance Texaco*.   (#17995)

LAST CHANCE TEXACO
(DRAMA)

By PETER MALONEY

3 women—Interior

Originally staged to great acclaim at NYC's famed Ensemble Studio Theatre, this is a haunting, lyrical play set in the American Garage, a Texaco station in a small Texas town run by a mother and her daughter. Late one night, while driving through, a city woman named Ruth has a flat tire, an occurrence which causes her own unusual life to intersect with Verna and Cissy, as they fix her tire in the American Garage. This play is an excellent source of monologue and scene material. It is also a gripping piece of theatre. Published with *Pastoral*.   (#13887)

BUSINESSMAN'S LUNCH
(COMEDY)

By MICHAEL QUINN

4 men, 1 woman—Interior

Originally produced by the famed Actors Theatre of Louisville, this marked the debut of a wonderful new comic playwriting voice. We are in one of those quiche-and-salad restaurants, where three high-powered young executives of a nearby candy company are having lunch as they discuss company politics and various marketing and advertising strategies. They particularly enjoy making fun of one of their fellows who is not present, whom they consider a hopeless nerd—until, that is, they learn that he is engaged to marry the boss's daughter. "Cleverly skewers corporate stereotypes."—NY Times.   (#4712)

Penguin Blues

by Ethan Phillips

Comic Drama. 1m., 1f. Int. This beautiful short play by actor Ethan Phillips of TV's "Benson" wowed them at Philadelphia Festival Theatre for New Plays. The critics were unanimous in their praise. We are in a room in an alcoholism rehabilitation center. The characters are Gordon, a manic alcoholic who knows the score, and Angelica, a nun who denies that she is an alcoholic. In the moving climax, Angelica finally recognizes why she is there; and in so doing, takes the painful first step towards sobriety. "One of the loveliest moments of emotional revelation I've seen in the theatre."—News of Delaware County.

(#18934)

Portfolio

by Tom Donaghy

Comedy. 1m., 1f., plus 1 offstage voice. Int. This amusing satire of advertising was produced to great audience mirth and critical approval at NYC's famed comedy theatre, Manhattan Punchline. We are on a photo shoot for a print ad campaign. The photographer, who is present only by voice, has had the brilliant idea to deck his model with live pigeons. He's hired a "pigeon man" to bring in a truckload of them. He becomes most annoyed, though, when the pigeons (which are mimed, by the way), won't take direction as easily as the model, much to the distress of the hapless pigeon man. Meanwhile, the model remains unflappable. In her business, she's used to anything and everything! (#18952)

Haiku

by Katherine Snodgrass

Drama. 3f., Int. This sublimely beautiful short play won the prestigious Heidemann Award given by the Actors Theatre of Louisville, perhaps the most important one-act play award in the United States. The story concerns a woman who lives with her retarded daughter, who has miraculously at brief intervals been "normal." In fact, the daughter, Louise, is sometimes super-normal, speaking in beautiful haiku poetry, which her mother has recorded and has had published under the mother's name. Then an older daughter, Billie, comes for a visit. Billie only knows her sister as hopelessly retarded, and refuses to believe that her mother's poetry has actually been composed by her sister. (#10650)

INCIDENT AT SAN BAJO
Drama
by Brad Korbesmeyer

3m., 4f. Bare Stage. The residents of a trailer camp at San Bajo have quite a story to tell, about a stranger who visited each one in turn, selling a mysterious elixir which he claimed would make them "live longer." Most of the residents of San Bajo did not buy the elixir of course—and they are now dead, the water supply having been poisoned by the mysterious stranger. Only seven are left to tell the tale—the seven who drank the elixir which, it turned out, was an antidote! Each tells his story in a series of interlocking monologues given to an unseen interviewer. The effect is somewhat like a "60 Minutes" segment, with an imaginary Morley Safer. This most unusual new play was the 1988 winner of Actors Theatre of Louisville's Heidemann Award, perhaps the most prestigious one-act play award in the United States.   (#11654)

BAIT AND SWITCH
Comedy
by Richard Dresser

3m., 2f. Int. Doug and Gary own and run a restaurant on the boardwalk which is fast going under, largely due to a recent influx of stinging jellyfish which has kept customers away from the beach, but also due to the fact that the two brothers are less than adept businessmen—particularly Gary, who isn't even aware that his brother is skimming profits. Their only hope is Kenny, a slick wiseguy with possible Mob connections. Kenny meets with Gary and Doug, sizes up the situation immediately, and eventually does take over the restaurant, forcing the two brothers out and, possibly, ending up with Gary's wife Lucy as part of the deal. Another incisive comic look at the American entrepreneurial mentality from the author of *The Downside, Better Days* and *Alone at the Beach.*   (#3948)

TONE CLUSTERS
Joyce Carol Oates
Drama

1m., 1f., plus 1 male voice. Bare stage. Frank and Emily Gulick are a nice middle-American couple with a nice house in a nice neighborhood. Why, then are they obviously under so much strain? As they are interviewed by an unseen interrogator, their story, and their predicament, emerges. The mutilated body of a 14 year-old girl from the neighborhood has been found in their basement, and their son is charged with the murder. Desperately, they cling to the belief that their son is not guilty, even as it becomes increasingly clear that he is the murderer. And, even as we are moved by the pitiable Gulicks, we ask ourselves, do they somehow share in the guilt of the crime? And: could we, as parents, someday find ourselves in their predicament? This extraordinary play by one of America's foremost women of letters won the prestigious Heideman Award bestowed by Actors Theatre of Louisville, which commissioned it and gave it its world premier at the famed Humana Festival. In *In Darkest America*.   (#22727)

THE ECLIPSE
Joyce Carol Oates
Drama

1m., 3f Int. Stephanie Washburn, a middle-aged college professor, lives with her mother Muriel in a small apartment in Philadelphia. Muriel was once a brilliant high school teacher. Now, she is retired, and her mind is going, possibly from Alzheimer's disease. As she goes in and out of reality, she makes her daughter's life miserable, even going so far as to call the local department of social services to accuse Stephanie of abusing her—a total fabrication, of course. Muriel also has a fantasy that she has a Latin lover, a Señor Rios, with whom she is carrying on a torrid affair. There is no Señor Rios, of course. Or is there? In the end, as flamenco music plays, Muriel enters, in a Spanish dancing dress, for her big date with Señor Rios, who appears, exactly as Muriel has described him, for a torrid dance with Muriel around the apartment as Stephanie sleeps in a chair, oblivious to it all. Then Muriel leaves for her date with the dark gentleman, and both women are finally released from their suffering. Death has finally claimed Muriel. This haunting play by one of America's foremost women of letters was commissioned by the Actors Theatre of Louisville, which produced it as part of their famed Humana Festival, and was subsequently produced Off Broadway in New York by Ensemble Studio Theatre. In *In Darkest America*.   (#7633)

STEAK NIGHT

Comedy
by Richard Polak

3m. 2f. Int. This is an amusing yet somewhat chilling look at an American family which is doing something about the so-called decline in family values. The family has a strict set of rules, and if you break one the other family members get to vote on the nature, length and severity of your punishment. The voting always takes place on the night the family has steak for dinner—sort of a family tradition, you might say. The most enthusiastic participant in this rite is Alan, a somewhat bullying 16-year-old; until, that is, he transgresses and the family votes on his punishment! Very cleverly, very deviously, Alan swings the vote in his favor and, in fact, takes over the family! "A dark little comedy with deepening layers ... provides a metaphor, both telling and chilling, of the ease with which a really determined, clever leader can and does use democracy to overthrow democracy ... playwright Polak combines grim Kafkaesque elements with a natural American embullience."—Drama-Logue.   (#21342)

TOTALLY COOL

Drama
by Jan Buttram

2m., 2f, to play 6m. 2f. Unit set. This terrific new drama depicts the relationship between two seemingly average teenage girls, Connie and Suzy, and shows how the two descend into destructive substance abuse. The play dramatizes both the emotional and physical consequences inherent in drug use. Both funny and sad, at times lighthearted and intense, *Totally Cool* mixes extreme realism and dream-like qualities to create a stirring and thought provoking experience. The dramatic landscape includes a variety of characters who help complete the story of Connie and Suzy; two paramedics, a pair of morgue attendants and the local medical examiner and his sidekick. (#22724)